In this book, the fifth in the TankCraft series on the Panther tank, we look at the first examples of this remarkable vehicle to go into combat during the summer of 1943. In the earlier books we described the reasons that led to the development of a medium tank armed with the Rheinmetall-Borsig 7.5cm KwK 42 gun and most readers will be aware of the Wehrmacht's need to counter the Russian T-34 and KV series of vehicles which the Panzers first encountered in 1941.

Unfortunately, reasons of space prevent a detailed examination of the Panther's development from the original proposal for a tank in the 30-ton class, the VK 30 project, to the first vehicles which left the assembly lines in January 1943, almost universally referred to today as the Panther ausführung D, usually abbreviated to ausf D. But it should be borne in mind that this initial production version, often described in contemporary documents as the Panther I, was essentially a research and development model, albeit one produced in large numbers. Rushed through the design stage with just a single complete prototype built (1), the first models to be assembled not only suffered from transmission failures and overheating engines but many of the armour plates of the hull and turrets simply did not fit.

Without exception the tanks allocated to Panzer-Abteilungen 51 and 52, the first Panther unit, and SS-Panzer-Regiment 1 were returned to the factories as unserviceable and these vehicles alone represent over 30 percent of the total production of the Panther ausf D. But by May 1943 the problems with construction had been remedied and the installation of the HL 230 P30 engine went so towards relieving the pressure transmission. At the same tim realised that the Panther II proje probably not continue (2) and in August 1943 the first true production version of the tank, the Panther ausf A, began to leave the manufacturing plants at Maschinenfabrik Niedersachen Hannover (MNH), followed with a month by Maschinenfabrik Augsburg-Nürnberg (MAN), Daimler-Benz and DEMAG.

Several sources have maintained that a Panther ausf B and Panther ausf C were at least under development but there is no real evidence to support this and the statements were probably based on assumptions made by Allied intelligence services during the war. Similarly, the suggestion that the Panther ausf D was named for the Daimler-Benz submissions in the initial 30-ton tank project cannot be supported as the prototype Versuchs-Panther series, eventually adopted as the production version, were built by MAN.

The first Panthers went into combat with Panzer-Regiment von Lauchert as part of Operation Citadel in July 1943 and although the tanks were hampered by mechanical problems they took a fearsome toll of the enemy, claiming the destruction of 263 Russian tanks for the loss of fifty-five Panthers in the space of ten days. Although it is these tanks which are the main focus of this book I have included the units which were equipped with the Panther and served on the Eastern Front up to the end of 1943 to provide a clearer picture of the history and development of what was one of the most potent weapons systems of the Second World War.

complete
2. A decision which was made official in June 1943.

The V2 Panther prototype built by Maschinenfabrik Augsburg-Nürnberg. The most obvious difference between this vehicle and the production Panther ausf D is the smaller turret with the bulge under the commander's cupola. There were many minor additions and these are described in the Technical Details and Modifications section of this book. Note the civilian number plate hanging from the hull glacis.

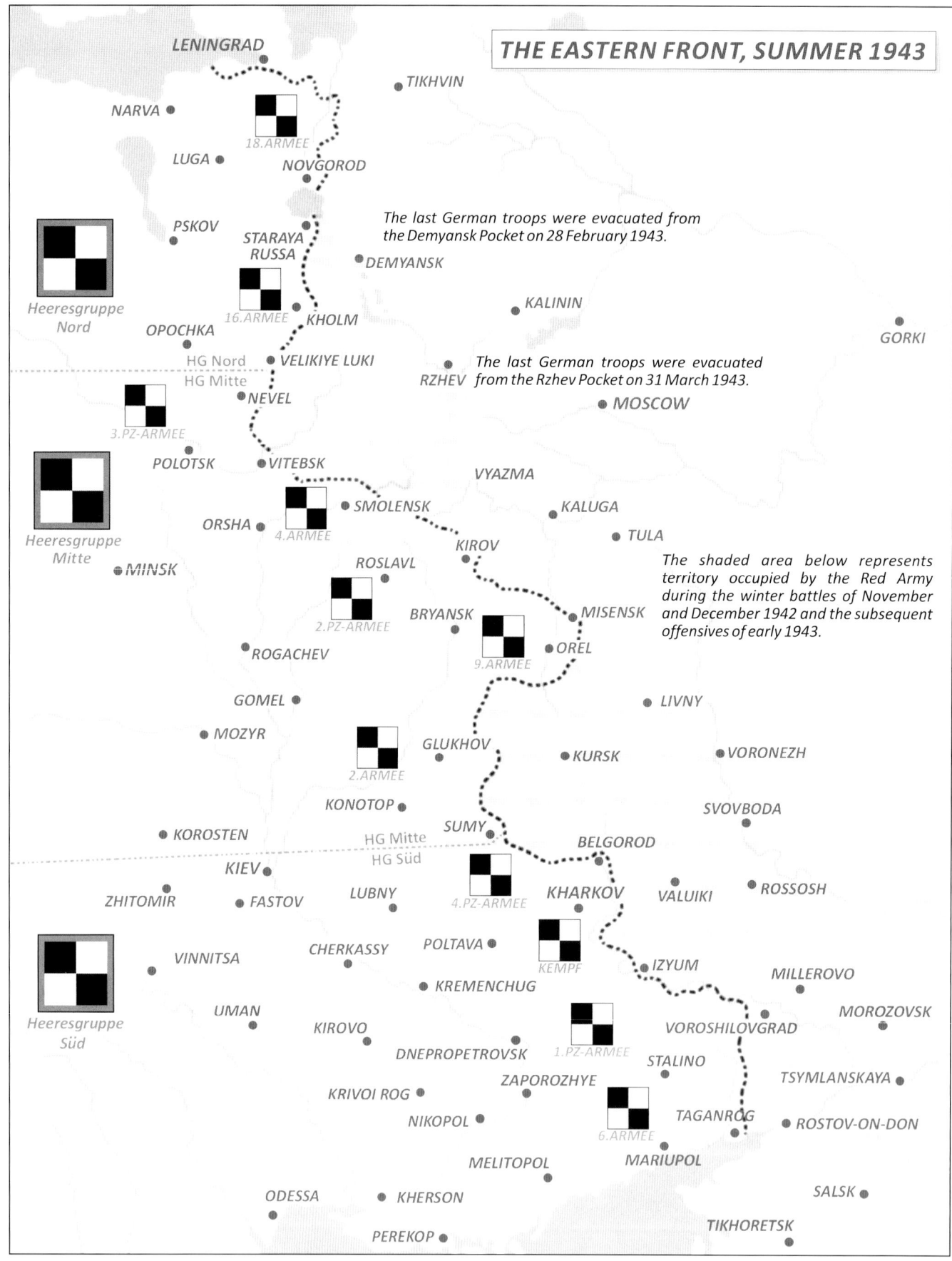

THE EASTERN FRONT, SUMMER 1943

The last German troops were evacuated from the Demyansk Pocket on 28 February 1943.

The last German troops were evacuated from the Rzhev Pocket on 31 March 1943.

The shaded area below represents territory occupied by the Red Army during the winter battles of November and December 1942 and the subsequent offensives of early 1943.

Heeresgruppe Nord

Heeresgruppe Mitte

Heeresgruppe Süd

18.ARMEE
16.ARMEE
3.PZ-ARMEE
4.ARMEE
2.PZ-ARMEE
9.ARMEE
2.ARMEE
4.PZ-ARMEE
KEMPF
1.PZ-ARMEE
6.ARMEE

HG Nord
HG Mitte
HG Mitte
HG Süd

LENINGRAD
TIKHVIN
NARVA
LUGA
NOVGOROD
PSKOV
STARAYA RUSSA
DEMYANSK
KALININ
GORKI
OPOCHKA
16.ARMEE KHOLM
VELIKIYE LUKI
RZHEV
MOSCOW
NEVEL
POLOTSK
VITEBSK
VYAZMA
ORSHA
SMOLENSK
KALUGA
TULA
MINSK
ROSLAVL
KIROV
BRYANSK
MISENSK
ROGACHEV
OREL
GOMEL
LIVNY
MOZYR
GLUKHOV
KURSK
VORONEZH
KONOTOP
SVOVBODA
KOROSTEN
SUMY
BELGOROD
KIEV
KHARKOV
VALUIKI
ROSSOSH
ZHITOMIR
FASTOV
LUBNY
POLTAVA
IZYUM
VINNITSA
CHERKASSY
MILLEROVO
KREMENCHUG
MOROZOVSK
UMAN
KIROVO
VOROSHILOVGRAD
DNEPROPETROVSK
STALINO
TSYMLANSKAYA
KRIVOI ROG
ZAPOROZHYE
NIKOPOL
TAGANROG
ROSTOV-ON-DON
MELITOPOL
MARIUPOL
ODESSA
KHERSON
SALSK
PEREKOP
TIKHORETSK

Our map shows the situation in the East on the eve of the German summer offensive, codenamed Operation Citadel, which commenced on 5 July 1943. By the spring of that year the Red Army had pushed the Germans back from the banks of the Don River, west of Stalingrad, entering the city of Kursk on 8 February and Kharkov, the second-largest city in the Ukraine, just over a week later. Although Kharkov was retaken in March the front line had been moved back in the south from the Caucasus Mountains to what is today central Ukraine and on the front of Heeresgruppe Nord the siege of Leningrad, which had been encircled since September 1941, had effectively been lifted by the end of January 1943. Employing the assets of two army groups, Operation Citadel was, however, dwarfed by the German offensive operations of 1941 and 1942 and it would be the last year of the war before the Wehrmacht mounted another large-scale attack in the East. The timeline shown on the following pages highlights the most important events of the period.

Abandoned along the Belogrod to Oboyan road in July 1943, this Panther ausf D of 8.Kompanie, Panzer-Abteilung 52 was one of thirty-one vehicles studied by the Russians after the fighting around Kursk. Another photograph of this tank is reproduced on page 52 were the technical details are discussed.

9 January 1943. *Panzer-Abteilung 51 (Panther) is created by renaming II.Abteilung, Panzer-Regiment 33. The battalion is transferred to Grafenwöhr in Germany to begin training on the new Panther tanks.*

2 February 1943. *Encircled since late November 1942, the last remnants of 6.Armee, holding out on the northern edge of Stalingrad, surrender to the Soviets.*

8 February 1943. *Red Army units take Kursk, an important road and rail junction between Voronezh and Kiev. On the next day Soviet troops enter Belgorod, near the present-day Ukrainian border.*

9 February 1943. *Panzer-Abteilung 52 (Panther) is formed from elements of I.Abteilung, Panzer-Regiment 15. The battalion goes into training, first at Erlagen in Germany then at Mailly-le-Camp in eastern France.*

12 February 1943. *On the Eastern Front, German troops evacuate Krasnodar and withdraw to defensive positions in the Kuban bridgehead. Within days Rostov-on-Don is captured by the Russians.*

16 February 1943. *Russian troops occupy parts of Kharkov, in modern-day Ukraine, after nine days of savage house-to-house fighting.*

18 February 1943. *Hitler arrives at the headquarters of Heeresgruppe Süd at Zaporozhye to be informed that Kharkov, less than 200 kilometres to the north, has been abandoned to the Soviets.*

21 February 1943. *A German counterattack, aimed at retaking Kharkov, commences.*

25 February 1943. *The Red Army launches a major offensive against the front of Heeresgruppe Mitte.*

1 March 1943. *A Russian offensive to the south of Leningrad pushes the Germans towards the west.*

7 March 1943. *After almost two weeks of bitter fighting the Russian assault against Heeresgruppe Mitte is called off and the Soviet units are redirected towards the German drive on Kharkov.*

11 March 1943. *Troops of SS-Panzergrenadier-Division Leibstandarte SS Adolf Hitler fight their way into the centre of Kharkov. By the evening none of the division's tanks are operational. On the following day German troops evacuate Vyazma on the Moscow to Smolensk highway.*

14 March 1943. *The Germans declare that Kharkov has been secured although sporadic fighting continues for two more days. Both sides are exhausted by the ceaseless combat and at about this time the spring rains commence, greatly impeding mobile operations. The German counterattack has been a spectacular tactical success but a large bulge has been created in the front around Kursk which extends deep into the German lines.*

22 March 1943. *German troops recapture Belgorod.*

8 April 1943. *The Soviet high command predicts that German personnel losses will force the Wehrmacht to rely principally on its armoured units and air assets in the coming spring and advises that strong anti-tank defences be created around the Kursk salient. This is precisely where Hitler has decided to attack.*

14 April 1943. *A limited German offensive to the south-east of Leningrad is repulsed. On the following day Hitler orders that planning commence for a major assault on the salient formed around the city of Kursk to be codenamed Unternehmen Zitadelle, or Operation Citadel. The attack is initially scheduled for early May.*

27 April 1943. *Generaloberst Walter Model, who is to command 9.Armee in the coming offensive, meets with Hitler to express his concerns about the Soviet defences around Kursk. Model's advice is that the assault should begin immediately or be postponed indefinitely. Generalfeldmarschall Manstein, the architect of the Kharkov counteroffensive, agrees with Model.*

4 May 1943. At a meeting in Munich Hitler advises his generals that Operation Citadel is to be postponed, countering Manstein's suggestion that the attack begin as soon as possible with the argument that a delay will allow the new Panther tanks to be deployed.

7 May 1943. Oberkommando der Wehrmacht (OKW) advises the commanders on the Eastern Front that Operation Citadel will commence on 12 June 1943.

10 May 1943. Generaloberst Guderian, the inspector-general of armoured troops, begs Hitler to abandon the coming offensive and conserve the Army's strength. Hitler continues to vacillate and the date for Citadel is again postponed to 20 June 1943.

26 May 1943. The Red Army begins an offensive against the German forces isolated in the Kuban bridgehead between the Sea of Azov and the Black Sea.

17 June 1943. The OKW Operations Staff advise Hitler to cancel the proposed offensive against the Kursk salient. Unconvinced, he postpones the commencement date yet again to 3 July 1943.

25 June 1943. The first elements of Panzer-Abteilungen 51 and 52 are unloaded at Bohodukhiv, west of Kharkov in modern-day Ukraine. Both battalions are placed under the command of Panzer-Regiment von Lauchert.

1 July 1943. Just two days before the assault on the Kursk salient is scheduled to begin, Hitler postpones the launch of Operation Citadel to Monday, 5 July 1943.

3 July 1943. Throughout the day Soviet aircraft attack the German units as they wait in their deployment areas on either flank of the Kursk salient.

4 July 1943. The last tanks of Panzer-Regiment von Lauchert arrive at the front and during the evening reach their jump-off positions between Moshchenoye and Tomorovka, west of Belgorod.

5 July 1943. At 4.30am Operation Citadel begins and immediately runs into trouble as massed Russian artillery accurately pounds the German positions. At 8.30am the tanks of Panzer-Regiment GD begin their attack followed by 184 Panthers of Panzer-Regiment von Lauchert. Although the first day's objective, the village of Tscherkasskoje, is reached by nightfall the Panthers are held up at the 80-metre-wide Berezovyi Ravine which is heavily mined and eighteen tanks are lost.

6 July 1943. With the tanks of Panzer-Regiment GD on their right flank, Major von Lauchert's Panthers push on towards the village of Lukhanino. Once again, the German tanks are held up by extensive minefields and stiff resistance. One of the thirty-seven Panthers lost on this day was disabled by a Pzkpfw IV of 11.Panzer-Division, killing the entire crew.

7 July 1943. The Panthers reach the village of Gremuchiy, south of Oboyan. As darkness falls Major von Lauchert reports that just twenty Panthers are operational with six of the day's casualties caused by engine fires.

8 July 1943. Major von Lauchert's Panthers push on towards Oboyan, engaging and destroying a number of Russian T-34 tanks at ranges of over 2,000 metres. By the end of the day II.SS-Panzerkorps, operating on the battalion's right, has broken through the second Soviet defensive line.

11 July 1943. Panzer-Regiment von Lauchert has lost thirty-one Panthers with a further 131 in need of repair. Many of the latter have been damaged by mines or enemy fire but over forty are unavailable due to mechanical failures. That night Kluge, the commander of Heeresgruppe Mitte, urges Hitler to call off the operation, but he refuses.

12 July 1943. Elements of Obergruppenführer Paul Hausser's II.SS-Panzerkorps advance to within sight of the village of Prokhorovka where a fierce tank battle ensues. Over the next three days Hausser's men, now joined by III.SS-Panzerkorps, attempt to push forward to Seversky Donets and encircle and destroy the Russian units they had faced at Prokhorovka but by 15 July, realise they can go no further.

A Panther ausf D of 1.Kompanie, Panzer-Abteilung 51 photographed in July 1943. The wooden stowage boxes on the hull rear were added to many, but not all, the tanks of Panzer-Regiment von Lauchert before they left Germany. The boxes could vary in size and sometimes only one was fitted. Note the armoured cover for the snorkel and submersible equipment just visible between the boxes. This is one of the few 1.Kompanie tanks to carry the panther's head marking which is just visible on the forward edge of the turret below the company number.

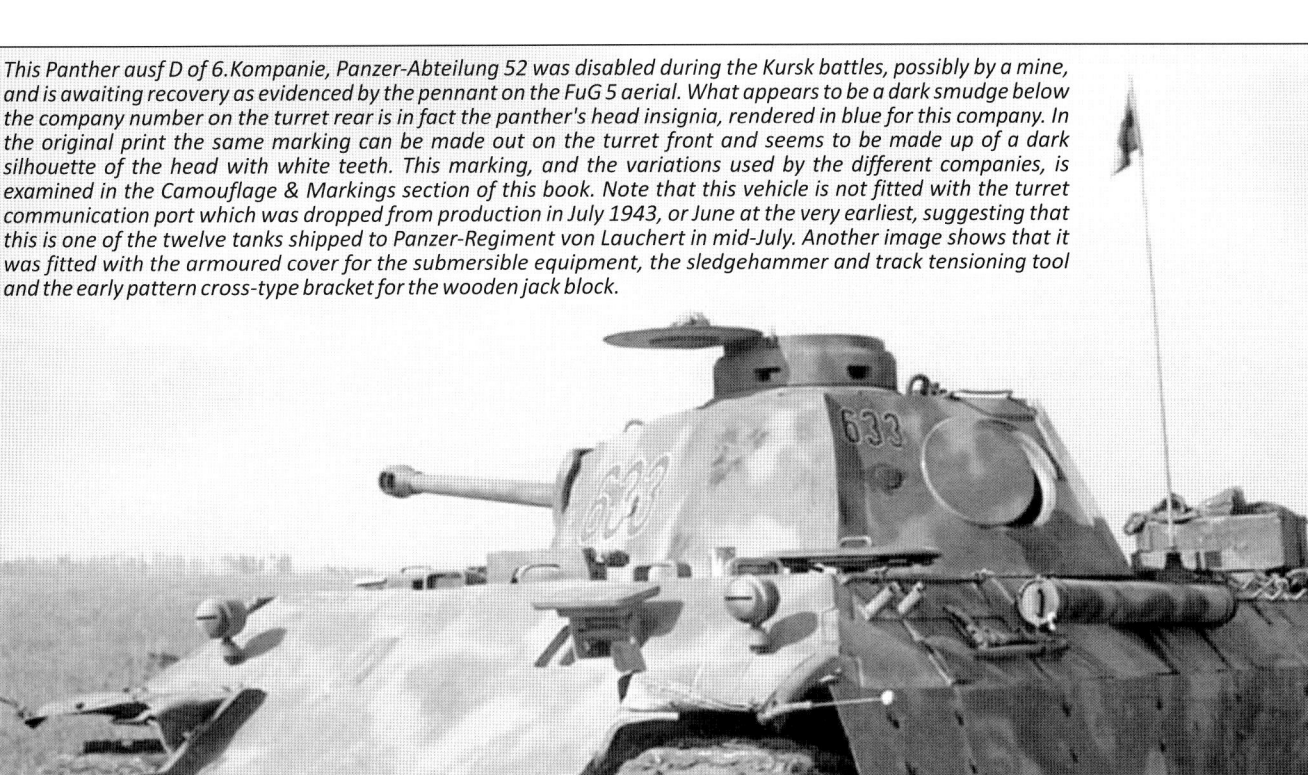

This Panther ausf D of 6.Kompanie, Panzer-Abteilung 52 was disabled during the Kursk battles, possibly by a mine, and is awaiting recovery as evidenced by the pennant on the FuG 5 aerial. What appears to be a dark smudge below the company number on the turret rear is in fact the panther's head insignia, rendered in blue for this company. In the original print the same marking can be made out on the turret front and seems to be made up of a dark silhouette of the head with white teeth. This marking, and the variations used by the different companies, is examined in the Camouflage & Markings section of this book. Note that this vehicle is not fitted with the turret communication port which was dropped from production in July 1943, or June at the very earliest, suggesting that this is one of the twelve tanks shipped to Panzer-Regiment von Lauchert in mid-July. Another image shows that it was fitted with the armoured cover for the submersible equipment, the sledgehammer and track tensioning tool and the early pattern cross-type bracket for the wooden jack block.

13 July 1943. A planned attack by the Panther tanks of Panzer-Regiment von Lauchert is cancelled due to a sudden downpour which renders resupply impossible. Later that day Hitler orders the suspension of Operation Citadel. The battle for the Kursk salient was an important victory for the Soviets and despite their obviously exaggerated claims the Germans have suffered severely.

14 July 1943. The Russians launch a massive counteroffensive south of Kursk against the units of 4.Panzerarmee and Armeeabteilung Kempf. By the end of the day Panzer-Regiment von Lauchert has twenty operational tanks and has completely run out of ammunition.

15 July 1943. The surviving Panthers of Panzer-Abteilung 51 are handed over to Panzer-Abteilung 52.

18 July 1943. The headquarters staff of Panzer-Brigade 10 and Major von Lauchert's surviving Panthers are detached from Panzergrenadier-Division GD and subordinated directly to XLVIII.Panzerkorps.

21 July 1943. A report prepared by 4.Panzerarmee states that forty-one operational Panther tanks are available at the front. A further eighty-five are in repair while sixteen were so badly damaged that they have been returned to Germany. A total of fifty-eight have been completely destroyed. Early the next day, in the sector of Heeresgruppe Nord, a massive artillery barrage heralds the start of the Third Battle of Lake Ladoga.

29 July 1943. In southern Ukraine, the Germans commence a series of counterattacks to improve their positions along the Mius River between Luhansk and Donetsk.

1 August 1943. Hitler orders the immediate evacuation of the Orel salient.

2 August 1943. Hitler orders that German units in the East are to hold their ground at any cost. But with the Russians continuing to gain ground around Orel Manstein adopts what he calls a 'flexible defence', effectively ignoring Hitler's order.

3 August 1943. The Red Army launches an offensive from the Belgorod area toward Poltava and Russian units are able to penetrate deep into the left flank of Heeresgruppe Süd, forcing the Germans to retreat.

4 August 1943. In the Ukraine the Red Army retakes Orel, forcing 9.Armee to withdraw towards Bryansk to avoid encirclement.

5 August 1943. The Russians take Orel and Belgorod and now threaten Kharkov.

12 August 1943. Belatedly, Hitler orders the construction of a fortified defensive work along the Dnieper River referred to as the Panther-Wotan Line. The Führer christens the defences the 'Ostwall' but many German commanders are so dismissive of the project that they refuse to use the name.

16 August 1943. The Red Army launches an offensive against the Mius River line toward Stalino.

19 August 1943. Panzer-Abteilung 52 is renamed I.Abteilung, Panzer-Regiment 15 and attached to 11.Panzer-Division.

22 August 1943. The Panthers of SS-Panzer-Regiment 2 go into action for the first time near Kharkov. Later that day the Germans abandon the city for the last time.

25 August 1943. The Russians continue their advance to the west of Kharkov.

31 August 1943. At the urging of Generalfeldmarschall Manstein, Hitler agrees to limited withdrawals in Ukraine.

6 September 1943. Russian units succeed in driving a wedge between Heeresgruppe Mitte and Heeresgruppe Süd. On the following day The Germans begin the evacuation of the Kuban bridgehead across the Strait of Kerch to the Crimea.

10 September 1943. The Russians recapture the Black Sea port of Novorossiysk.

12 September 1943. The Panthers of 2.Kompanie, SS-Panzer-Regiment 2, supported by three assault guns, claim the destruction of at least twenty-eight Soviet tanks in a skirmish fought near Nikolajewka. The company commander, Hauptsturmführer Friedrich Holzer, was later awarded the Ritterkreuz for his leadership and bravery.

17 September 1943. Red Army units capture Bryansk, about 300 kilometres south-west of Moscow.

19 September 1943. A Kampfgruppe made up of the Panthers of Panzer-Regiment 23 and infantrymen of 16.Panzergrenadier-Division capture Slavjanka in southern Ukraine, cutting off two Soviet armoured corps. Oberst Joachim Sander, the commander of the Panzer regiment, is later awarded the Ritterkreuz, becoming one of just five soldiers of the regiment to receive the medal.

20 September 1943. The divisions of Heeresgruppe Süd begin to withdraw towards the Melitopol-Zaporozhye defensive line but Russian armoured spearheads cut them off near Dnepropetrovsk.

23 September 1943. In one week the Soviets take Poltava, Roslavl and Temryuk on the Black Sea coast. By the end of September the Russian bridgehead on the west bank of the Dnieper River is over 400 kilometres long.

6 October 1943. The Russians take Nevel, near the present-day Belarus border, driving a wedge between Heeresgruppe Nord and Heeresgruppe Mitte.

13 October 1943. The Russians reach the outskirts of Melitopol in southern Ukraine. On the following day German forces evacuate the Zaporozhye bridgehead on the eastern bank of the Dnieper River.

16 October 1943. Red Army units launch an offensive from the Bukryn bridgehead south of Kiev in an attempt to cut off the divisions of 1.Panzerarmee. After four days of savage fighting the Russians are repulsed with heavy losses.

23 October 1943. After a ten-day battle the Soviets finally take Melitopol. On the same day the city of Dnepropetrovsk, present-day Dnipro, is captured and advance Russian units push on to Krivoi Rog, over 100 kilometres to the west.

1 November 1943. German units in the Crimea are completely cut off.

6 November 1943. A massive Russian offensive succeeds in capturing Kiev and scattering the divisions of 4.Panzerarmee.

12 November 1943. Soviet units take Zhitomir, extending the Kiev bridgehead to a width of almost 300 kilometres.

14 November 1943. A counterattack near the town of Novo Ivanivka led by the Panthers of 8.Kompanie, Panzer-Regiment 23 succeeds in driving the Russians back and destroying thirty-one enemy tanks. Oberleutnant Gerhard Fischer, the company commander, is later awarded the Ritterkreuz for his actions on this day.

16 November 1943. The Panther tanks of Panzer-Regiment 1 go into action for the first time near Skvyra, south-west of Kiev. Although Zhitomir is recaptured in the following days, many of the tanks fall out due to mechanical failures.

20 November 1943. Red Army units achieve a breakthrough near Kremenchug, north-west of Dnepropetrovsk.

26 November 1943. The last elements of Heeresgruppe Mitte evacuate Gomel in southern Belarus.

30 November 1943. I.Abteilung, Panzer-Regiment 31, with seventy-six Panthers, is ordered to the Eastern Front.

13 December 1943. Heeresgruppe Mitte becomes engaged in a series of heavy defensive battles in the area around Vitebsk in north-eastern Belarus.

21 December 1943. The commander of I.Abteilung, SS-Panzer-Regiment 1 reports that since the battalion had returned to the Eastern Front in early November a total of twenty-one Panthers have been lost.

22 December 1943. While supporting an attack made by elements of 3.Fallschirmjäger-Division, six Panthers of I.Abteilung, Panzer-Regiment 31 are lost due to internal fires.

30 December 1943. A Russian offensive, undertaken by sixty-three divisions, captures Berdichev, south of Zhitomir.

Panther ausf D tanks of 3.Kompanie, Panzer-Abteilung 51 photographed at some time after August 1943 when the battalion was tactically subordinated to Panzergrenadier-Division Grossdeutschland, possibly near Karachev. At around this time the smaller turret numbers and the stalking panther insignia were adopted. Note that two pieces of the hull Schürzen have been removed and placed behind the exhaust mufflers, probably in an attempt to deflect the heat that these generated. Both tanks have the 16-bolt roadwheels, early cupola and tracks without Stollen suggesting that they are two of the original vehicles that arrived in early July 1943 with Panzer-Regiment von Lauchert.

The first units equipped with the Panther tank were the semi-independent battalions raised specifically for Operation Citadel in January and February 1943. In the following months a number of battalions and companies were detached from their parent regiments and returned to Germany to train on the new tanks and by 14 June 1943 the Oberkommando des Heeres (OKH) ordered that each Panzer battalion fighting in the East would be furnished with ninety-six tanks and that the majority of Panzer divisions would receive a battalion of the new Panther tanks by the end of the year.

As production increased, and the Panther II programme was shelved, orders for the uniform reorganisation of the Panzer divisions were issued on 24 September 1943 stipulating that each Panzer regiment's first battalion would be equipped with Panthers organised into a headquarters company and four tank companies (1).

Listed here are the battalions that were equipped with the Panther and served in the East during 1943 and I should mention that in this book, unlike the previous titles in this series, I have listed the units in the order in which they were returned to the front.

Panzer-Abteilung 51. The battalion was formed on 9 January 1943 from II.Abteilung, Panzer Regiment 33, which had been detached from 9.Panzer-Division. Hauptmann Heinrich Ernst Meyer, who had commanded the regiment's II.Abteilung throughout 1942, was chosen to lead the new battalion.

By 22 February 1943 a total of twenty Panthers had been received from the January and February production runs and one tank which was assembled in the first days of March (2). From the very start these vehicles displayed major technical deficiencies such as oil leaks, malfunctioning fuel pumps and transmission failures that led in some cases to internal fires.

On Thursday, 8 April 1943 an order from OKH directed the battalion to hand over all its tanks to I.Abteilung, Panzer-Regiment 1 and to leave Grafenwöhr for Truppenübungsplatz Mailly-le-Camp, a large training facility east of Paris. The battalion remained in France for just over a month and then returned to Grafenwöhr where ninety-six new Panther ausf D tanks were taken over by the end of May. But these too were plagued by various mechanical problems and all were sent to

............text continued on page 10

Notes

1. Circumstances dictated that this was sometimes the second battalion, as mentioned in the text.

2. Fahrgestelle Nummern (Fgst Nr.), or chassis numbers, 210001-210013, 210015, 210016, 211011, 211002, 211004-211006 and 213001.

A Panther ausf D of 4.Kompanie, Panzer-Abteilung 51 accompanied by a Pzkpfw III tank of Panzer-Regiment Grossdeutschland photographed near the Gremuchiy River north of Orel in the first days of Operation Citadel. The Panther has neither the rectangular stowage locker fitted to many of the battalion's tanks at Grafenwöhr nor the sledgehammer and track tensioning tool incorporated into production in June 1943 and fitted to the hull side.

PANZER-REGIMENT VON LAUCHERT, JULY 1943

All units of the German Army were organised using detailed tables of establishment known as Kriegsstärkenachweisung, usually abbreviated to KstN. These lists gave the full personnel and equipment allowance for a particular unit and were referred to by a number and date. The latter was all-important as some numbers were duplicated. It should be remembered that establishments were the ideal and rarely acheived in practice and that some KstN were temporarily amended to suit a particular unit. Where this is the case I have tried to make it clear. As mentioned in the text, the regimental headquarters was formed from Stab, Panzer-Regiment 39 and in addition to the tanks shown here also contained four Bergepanther recovery vehicles, two Sdkfz 250/1 halftracks and four Sdkfz 251/8 armoured ambulances, the latter with a Sanitäts-Zug or medical section.

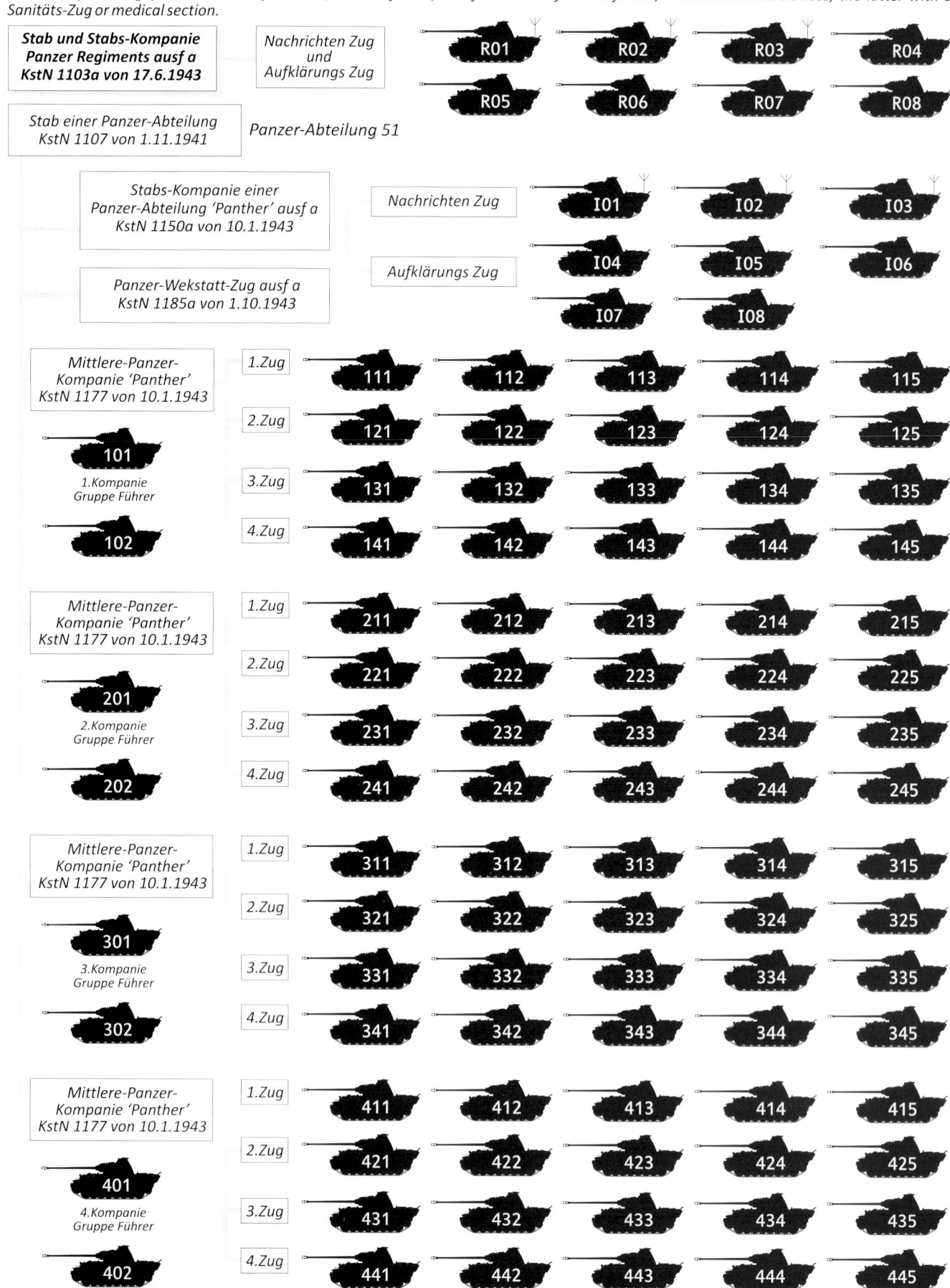

Although the surviving Oberkommando des Heeres (OKH) order which created Panzer-Abteilung 52 is not clear regarding the exact establishment of the battalion, the January 1943 order relating to the formation of Panzer-Abteilung 51 gives the Kriegsstärkenachweisungen to be used and we can reasonably assume that the two formations were organised identically. The eventual on-hand figures, as shown here, varied considerably and there is no obvious reason why this may have been so. The official allocation for KstN 1107 was six tanks with an organic maintenance unit while each company, organised according to KstN 1177, was supposed to be made up of a command troop of three tanks and four platoons of four tanks each. But the Heereswaffenamt allocation lists and unit diaries are quite clear and the numbers presented in our chart are accurate with each battalion having a total of ninety-six Panthers. Although somewhat speculative, the use of the 900 series of numbers for the battalion headquarters of Panzer-Abteilung 52 is partly confirmed by photographic evidence. One of these tanks is shown and discussed further in the Camouflage & Markings section of this book.

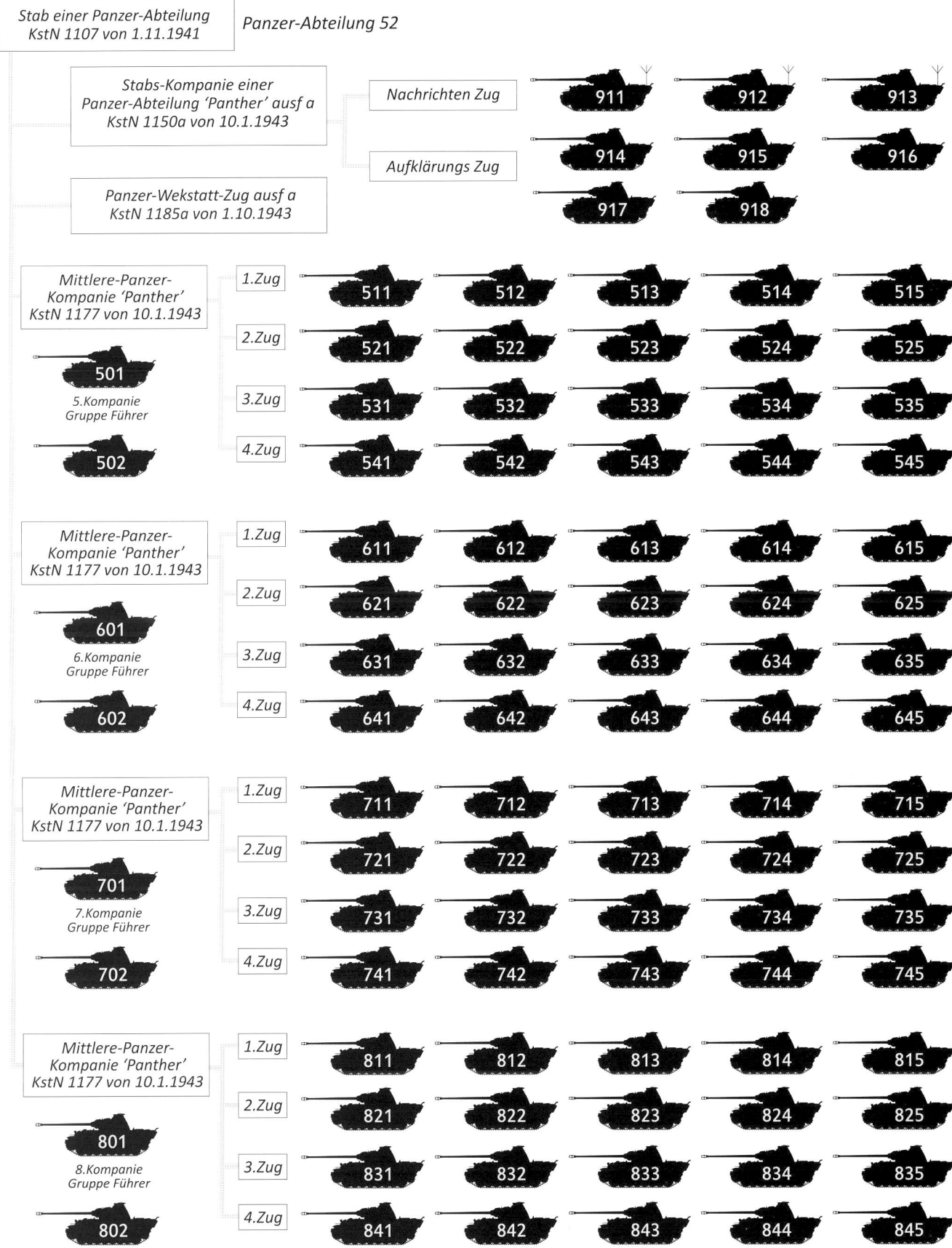

............*text continued from page 7*

Notes

1. The modified vehicles were all shipped from the Heereszeugamt on 17 and 18 June 1943.

2. In many accounts Rittmeister von Sivers' rank is given as Major but he was not promoted until October 1943. He had previously served with Panzer-Regiment 24 which retained the cavalry titles of rank, Rittmeister being the term used to denote a captain. Hauptmann Baumunk had been attached to Panzertruppenschule I at Erlangen.

DEMAG plant at Falkensee as part of the major modification and repair programme that was undertaken at that time. By 25 June 1943 the last of the repaired Panthers had been returned, as well as two Bergepanther recovery tanks, and on the same day the battalion began moving to the East (1).

The battalion took part in Operation Citadel as part of Panzer-Regiment von Lauchert, losing thirty-one Panthers as total write-offs. On 15 July 1943 the battalion was ordered to hand over its remaining tanks to Panzer-Abteilung 52 and was withdrawn to Gomel and then to Bryansk and three days later ninety-six new tanks were shipped from the Heereszeugamt (HZA). From 24 July 1943 the battalion was tactically subordinated to the headquarters of Panzergrenadier-Division Grossdeutschland (GD) and took part in the defensive battles between Dnipro and Krivoi Rog, present-day Kryvyi Rih in southern Ukraine. In the first week of January 1944 the battalion reverted to its former title of II.Abteilung, Panzer-Regiment 33 and returned to 9.Panzer-Division. See also Panzer-Regiment von Lauchert, below.

Panzer-Abteilung 52. This unit was raised from elements of I.Abteilung, Panzer-Regiment 15 on 9 February 1943. As part of 11.Panzer-Division the regiment had been in almost continuous front-line service during 1942 and had lost all its tanks by the end of that year. The battalion was initially commanded by Rittmeister Karl von Sivers but he fell ill while the tank crews were completing their training at Grafenwöhr, just days before the Panthers left for Russia, and was replaced by Hauptmann Georg Baumunk (2).

On 8 April 1943 the battalion was ordered from Erlangen in Germany to Truppenübungsplatz Mailly-le-Camp in France but the last crew members did not arrive in France until the end of the month and within days the battalion was transferred to the Grafenwöhr training grounds. During the last two weeks of May 1943 the battalion received ninety-six Panthers but these were all found to be mechanically unreliable and sent to the Falkensee plant to be repaired and modified. On 24 June 1943, still without any tanks, the battalion was advised that it would soon be moved to the East and combined with Panzer-Abteilung 51. Five days later the last of ninety-six completely new Panthers had arrived at Grafenwöhr for the battalion and on the same day the tanks began leaving for the front. The last elements of Panzer-Abteilung 52 to arrive on the Eastern Front were unloaded east of Poltava on 4 July 1943, the day before Operation Citadel commenced.

The battalion took part in Operation Citadel as part of Panzer-Regiment von Lauchert, losing twenty-four Panthers completely destroyed and a further four which had to be returned to Germany for extensive repairs. On 15 July 1943 the battalion absorbed the remaining tanks of Panzer-Abteilung 51 and as many as five Panthers from the headquarters of Panzer-Regiment von Lauchert when it returned to Germany in the first week of August. The battalion operated in support of 11.Panzer-Division for some weeks and on 19 August 1943 the few remaining tanks and crews were incorporated into I.Abteilung, Panzer-Regiment 15, the unit from which it had originally been formed. See also Panzer-Regiment von Lauchert, below.

A Panther ausf D of 7.Kompanie, Panzer-Abteilung 52 photographed during the first days of Operation Citadel. Note the extended fender and width indicators. Both these features were standard fittings but many were quickly lost or damaged in service. The panther's head insignia is just visible in front of the company number.

Although these photographs are of mediocre quality I have included both as they show tanks of the headquarters of Panzer-Regiment von Lauchert which had a maximum of just eight tanks on hand at any time. Most sources claim that these two Panther ausf D vehicles, both numbered R04, are the same tank but they are in fact different. Other images of the tank depicted at right show that it was fitted with the second pattern drive sprocket, was missing one headlight and lacked the smoke candle dischargers. On closer examination it is also obvious that the number is rendered in a different style.

Note also that the tank shown at left is a Befehlspanzerwagen and the armoured cover for the FuG 8 antenna insulator is visible on the rear hull while the FuG 5 antenna can be seen on the turret roof to the left of the commander's cupola. The Panther shown above is fitted with one of the large wooden stowage boxes which were an identifying feature of the tanks of this regiment. It is possible that this tank was disabled in the early stages of Operation Citadel and replaced by the Befehlspanzerwagen shown at left.

Panzer-Regiment von Lauchert. Formed around the headquarters staff of Panzer-Regiment 39, which had been detached from 17.Panzer-Division in late April 1943, the regiment also contained Panzer-Abteilungen 51 and 52 and was commanded by Major Meinrad von Lauchert, an experienced and highly-decorated officer who had served in the Polish and French campaigns.

From late May 1943 the tank crews of the headquarters staff were trained on the Panther at Erlangen in Germany and on 20 June the unit was directed to be organised according to KstN 1103a von 17.6.1943 Stab eines Panzer-Regiments and be ready for deployment within two days (1).

On 25 June 1943 Panzer-Abteilungen 51 and 52 were subordinated to the command of Stab/Panzer-Regiment 39 which was from that date referred to as Panzer-Regiment von Lauchert. The regiment's title is mentioned in OKH orders and also the recommendations for Major von Lauchert's awards of the German Cross in Gold and the Oakleaves to his Ritterkreuz. In some official documents this formation is referred to as Panzer-Regiment (Panther) von Lauchert and together with Panzer-Regiment GD, Major von Lauchert's regiment formed Panzer-Brigade 10 (2).

On 5 July 1943 Operation Citadel was launched and the regiment, following the tanks of Panzer-Regiment GD, managed to break through the first line of Soviet defences and capture the towns of Cherkasskoye and Jaoki by the end of the first day. Heavy fighting continued for the next few days with the Panthers advancing on both sides of the Yakovlevo to Oboyan road north of Belgorod and clearing the immediate area of Russian forces. But by Saturday, 10 July 1943 Major von Lauchert reported that just ten of his tanks were serviceable and on the following Monday the Soviets mounted a strong counterattack near Verkhopenye. Although the enemy were beaten back, a sudden downpour, which lasted for most of the next day, rendered the ground largely impassable and on 15 July 1943 Operation Citadel was call off. On the same day Panzer-Abteilung 51 was ordered to hand over all its surviving tanks to Panzer-Abteilung 52 and the crews were moved to Gomel in present-day Belarus and came under the direct command of Heeresgruppe Mitte.

On 28 July 1943, Panzer-Abteilung 52 was detached from the regiment and tactically subordinated to 11.Panzer-Division while the headquarters staff was transferred to St Pölten in Austria and attached to Panzer-Ersatz-Abteilung 33, handing over their remaining vehicles to Panzer-Regiment 15 (3).

Panzer-Regiment 15. Originally raised in 1937, the regiment was attached to 11.Panzer-Division in September 1940 in the reorganisation that followed the French Campaign. In February 1943, I.Abteilung was used to form Panzer-Abteilung 52, one of the first Panther units, mentioned above.

On 19 August 1943 the few remaining tanks of Panzer-Abteilung 52 were integrated into Panzer-Regiment 15 as the regiment's I.Abteilung and in this way returned to 11.Panzer-Division (4). In mid-September 1943 the battalion reported that a total of ninety-six Panthers were on hand, a full allocation, but that forty-eight

Notes

1. This was an interim establishment created to facilitate the combat debut of the Panther.

2. Panzer-Brigade 10 was purely a command and control formation with no tanks of its own. In the autumn of 1943 the personnel were transferred to France and used to form Panzer-Ausbildungs Stab 2, a training unit.

3. This only included the surviving tanks, the number of which is unknown but may have been five. The headquarters staff arrived in St Pölten with nine lorries, twenty cars, two motorcycles and ten mules. The latter were certainly not mentioned in KstN 1103a.

4. There is some confusion about the exact dates as the battalion had been operating with 11.Panzer-Division since 28 July 1943.

Notes

1. Although a number of the Waffen-SS formations underwent several name changes during their existence, the titles used here, as a matter of convenience, are those that were current during the summer of 1943.

of these were in either short or long-term repair. The battalion took part in the fighting along the Dnieper river at Cherkassy and Krivoi Rog, eventually falling back towards the present-day Moldovan border.

In December the division was attached to LII.Armeekorps and supported the paratroopers of 2.Fallschirmjäger-Division and Panzer-Regiment 31 in the defence of Kirovograd, modern-day Kropyvnytskyi in Ukraine. On the last day of 1943 the battalion reported that just six tanks were fully operational.

SS-Panzer-Regiment 2. Created in October 1942, this formation was attached to SS-Panzergrenadier-Division Das Reich (1). On Saturday, 1 May 1943 the regiment's I.Abteilung was transferred to Germany to be re-equipped with Panther tanks and the first sixteen vehicles arrived in the following June. An additional fifty-five tanks were allocated on 2 August 1943, although it is not certain when these were actually delivered, and before the end of the month I.Abteilung had returned to the front where the regiment's parent division was fighting to hold on to Kharkov. With the fall of the city, German units in the area pulled back across the Dnieper River and on 1 September the regiment reported that sixty-six Panthers were on hand, with twenty-one of those being fully operational, suggesting that five tanks had been completely destroyed.

By the end of September 1943 the Panthers were involved in the attacks made against the Soviet bridgehead on the west bank of the Dnieper near the village of Hrebeni, about 50 kilometres south of Kiev in modern-day Ukraine. The battles here were particularly fierce and by 5 October 1943 the battalion had just fifty-three Panthers on hand of which just one was considered serviceable. By December 1943, after almost continuous action, SS-Panzer-Regiment 2 had been reduced to a weak battalion made up of three companies equipped with just four serviceable Panthers, six Pzkpfw IV tanks and the remaining Tigers of the regiment's heavy company.

Panzer-Regiment 23. In mid-April 1943 the second battalion of Panzer-Regiment 201, which had been attached to 23.Panzer-Division since December 1941, returned to Germany and began its conversion to Panther tanks. Between 12 and 16 August a total of ninety-six new tanks were shipped from the HZA and at the same time the battalion was renamed II.Abteilung, Panzer-Regiment 23.

On 28 August 1943 the battalion, under Hauptmann Fritz Fechner, returned to the front but could not rejoin its parent division and was instead attached directly to XVII.Armeekorps which was attempting to defend Makiivka, today a suburb of Donetsk. The Panthers went into action for the first time on 4 September 1943 in support of 306.Infanterie-Division which was holding the present-day Kirovsky district on the western edge of Donetsk, blunting a Soviet attack without loss. But mechanical problems continued to hamper the performance of the Panther tanks and after an action near Fedorovka on 12 September 1943, fourteen disabled tanks that could not be recovered had to be destroyed by their own crews. In this same battle, the tanks of Kampfgruppe Fechner were unsuccessful in closing the gap the Russians had managed to create

This Panther ausf D of 4.Kompanie, SS-Panzer-Regiment 2 is probably one of the fifty-five tanks the regiment received in August 1943, just before returning to the Eastern Front. Note the ring for the anti-aircraft machine gun on the commander's cupola and the single headlight. Ernst Barkmann, who would later become famous for his actions during the Normandy campaign, was photographed in the turret of this tank and it is often incorrectly assumed that he was the commander.

A Panther ausf D of 2.Kompanie, Panzer-Regiment 15 photographed in the late autumn of 1943. The remaining tanks of Panzer-Abteilung 52 were incorporated into this regiment in late August and this tank is fitted with the wooden stowage boxes on the rear hull which were a feature of that battalion's Panthers. But items such as the single headlight, later drive sprocket, cupola anti-aircraft machine-gun ring and coating of Zimmerit suggest that this may be one of the eleven new tanks shipped from the Heereszeugamt between 15 and 19 October 1943. Note the bracket welded to the turret side to support the cupola hatch.

between 6.Armee and 1.Panzerarmee north of Pokrovsk, although Fechner was awarded the Ritterkreuz for his efforts.

By 15 September 1943 the battalion was returned to 23.Panzer-Division and although ten replacement tanks were received in October, by late December 1943 the battalion had been reduced to a strength of six Panthers. These tanks were handed over to 4.Kompanie, Panzer-Regiment 23 and II.Abteilung received an allocation of seventy-eight new tanks, the last of which arrived on 4 January 1944.

Panzer-Regiment 2. This formation was one of the pre-war regiments and in the reorganisation following the 1940 French campaign it was attached to 16.Panzer-Division. Completely destroyed in the battles for Stalingrad, the division was reformed in mid-February 1943 with a Panzer regiment made up of three battalions.

In May 1943, I.Abteilung was transferred to Bamberg in Germany while the other battalions, with the regimental headquarters, were sent to Italy. The battalion remained at Bamberg until late August when the crews were moved to Grafenwöhr and during the first two weeks of September seventy-one Panthers were shipped from the Heereszeugamt. Photographs would suggest that most of these were Panther ausf A models but a number of Panther ausf D tanks were on hand with the battalion's third and fourth companies and the headquarters.

On 30 September 1943 the battalion commander, Hauptmann Friedhelm Bollert, received the order that the Panthers would be moved to the Eastern Front immediately and the first tanks were loaded onto railway cars on the following morning. The battalion was attached to 17.Panzer-Division and took part in the defensive battles along the Dnieper River between Melitopol and Odessa where most of the tanks were lost by the end of November, many because they had broken down and could not be recovered.

In December 1943 seventy-six completely new tanks were allocated and it would be safe to assume that most of these, if not all, were Panther ausf A models (1). The battalion was involved in the fighting at Zlobin, in modern-day Belarus, and later around Shepetivka in northern Ukraine and in the first weeks of January 1944 rejoined 16.Panzer-Division.

Panzer-Regiment 1. Formed in October 1935, this unit served with 1.Panzer-Division. Plans to provide the division with a Panther battalion were first put forward as early as December 1942 but it was April 1943 before the regiment's I.Abteilung could train on the new tank and these were vehicles which Panzer-Abteilung 51 had deemed unserviceable. In May the division, less I.Abteilung, moved to Greece and in the following month it was decided that the battalion should be outfitted with Pzkpfw IV tanks and a platoon of Pzkpfw III flamethrowers (2).

In September 1943, I.Abteilung rejoined the division, which was now operating in western Croatia, and took part in anti-partisan operations. On 22 October 1943 the division was ordered to the Eastern Front and the tank crews of I.Abteilung were to report to Altengrabow in Germany to be completely re-equipped with Panther tanks.

Notes

1. In some sources the number of tanks allocated in September is given as sixty-two with fifty for December. Although the HZA allocation lists clearly show seventy-one and seventy-six respectively there are no delivery dates mentioned and so the lower figures are possible.

2. This was apparently viewed as a temporary expedient only as a number of tank crews were held at the Grafenwöhr training grounds with the intention that they would eventually be equipped with the Panther.

Notes

1. Nachschub Ost was the army's supply directorate in the East.

2. A further six tanks, taken from the same source, arrived towards the end of the month.

By 6 November 1943 the battalion had received seventy-six Panthers, including two Panzerbefehlswagen command tanks, and by the second week of the month the tanks had all been transported to Kozyatyn, in central Ukraine south-east of Berdychiv. The tanks were sent straight into action and took part in the recapture of Zhitomir but by the beginning of December just twenty-three tanks were operational. Tellingly, only three Panthers had been lost to enemy action while a total of fifty were awaiting repair.

During December 1943 the Panthers, with parts of Panzergrenadier-Regiment 113 and Panzer-Artillerie-Regiment 73, formed Kampfgruppe Bradel, an ad-hoc unit that fought in the battles around the city of Radomyshl, east of Zhitomir, in support of SS-Panzer-Regiment 1. Twenty-two new tanks were shipped to the battalion on 26 December 1943 directly from Nachschub Ost (1) and all had arrived during the first two weeks of January 1944.

SS-Panzer-Regiment 1. Built around SS-Panzer-Abteilung 1 in October 1942, the regiment was attached to SS-Panzergrenadier-Division LAH. On 1 May 1943 the regiment's I.Abteilung was ordered to convert to Panthers and returned to Germany to be re-equipped with the new tanks. The first forty vehicles were received during the following month and another thirty-one Panthers were delivered in July and all were early production Panther ausf D models. At the same time a large number of experienced officers and NCOs were transferred to SS-Panzer-Regiment 12.

From August 1943 the units of SS-Panzergrenadier-Division LAH, which had been fighting on the Eastern Front, were transferred to northern Italy and were soon after joined by I.Abteilung, SS-Panzer-Regiment 1. This battalion was apparently one of a number of Panther units to be organised using modified versions of KstN 1150a and KstN 1177 which lacked the Aufklärungs-Zug and had only seventeen tanks in each company, giving a total of seventy-one Panthers. By the end of November 1943 these vehicles had all been returned and a total of ninety-six new tanks, a full allocation, were shipped from the HZA.

The regiment returned to the East in November and after the heavy fighting between Cherkassy and Berdychiv in what is today northern Ukraine, SS-Panzer-Regiment 1 was reduced to the strength of a weak battalion-sized Kampfgruppe made up of three companies equipped with the surviving Tigers, Panthers and Pzkpfw IV tanks. See also Panzer-Abteilung (Panther/Bo.)Nord, below.

Panzer-Regiment 29. Formed on 1 October 1940 with three battalions, the regiment was attached to 12.Panzer-Division. In November 1943 personnel from the regiment's I.Abteilung were assigned to Heeresgruppe Nord as crews for a number of dug-in Panthers. See Panzer-Abteilung (Panther/Bo.)Nord, below.

Panzer-Regiment 31. Formed in August 1939, the regiment, made up of two battalions, was assigned to 5.Panzer-Division. On 5 May 1943 the regiment's I.Abteilung returned to Germany to begin its conversion to the Panther tank but did not receive any vehicles until mid-October and as late as 17 November 1943 most of the tanks allocated were in need of extensive modifications.

But by the end of November the Inspekteur der Panzertruppen reported to Hitler that the battalion was ready to return to the front and would probably be deployed with 20.Panzer-Division which was defending the area around Vitebsk, modern-day Viciebsk in Belarus. On 30 November 1943 the battalion arrived on the Eastern Front and was subordinated to 11.Panzer-Division which was at that time operating around modern-day Kropyvnytskyi on the west bank of the Dnieper River. The battalion remained here for the rest of the year, supporting 2.Fallschirmjäger-Division, reporting on 31 December 1943 that just nine Panthers were ready for combat.

Panzer-Abteilung (Panther/Bo.)Nord. On 1 November 1943 Hitler demanded of the Inspekteur der Panzertruppen that a Panther unit be made available to reinforce the Leningrad Front, particularly the area along the Neva Bay between modern-day St Petersburg and the Kronstadt naval base. As any armoured vehicles were in short supply at this time it was suggested that Panther tanks in need of repair or modification be employed as static defence points. No dedicated maintenance elements were allocated and OKH emphasised that the tanks were not to be cannibalised to produce fully operational vehicles. Further, where tanks were capable of movement this was to be kept to a minimum and offensive operations of any kind were not to be attempted.

The Panthers would be accompanied to the front by trained personnel from Panzer-Ersatz-Abteilung 33 who would pass on their knowledge to crews drawn from a number of Panzerjäger units under the control of Heeresgruppe Nord and then return to Germany. A total of fifty-four Pzkpfw V Panther ausf D tanks were shipped by 3 November 1943, taken over from SS-Panzer-Regiment 1 (2).

............text continued on page 16

The images reproduced on this page show tanks of I.Abteilung, SS-Panzer-Regiment 1 photographed near Reggio Emilia, north-east of Modena, in August or September 1943. All are Panther ausf D versions confirming that the original allocations were on hand in Italy. The vehicles shown in this image are from 2.Kompanie and those at the bottom of the page are from 1.Kompanie. The tanks were identified by a system of large red numbers outlined in white with the letter S, and possibly A, followed by a two-digit number denoting the headquarters vehicles.

Confusingly, I.Abteilung was referred to as the regiment's Schwere, or heavy, battalion although 13.Kompanie, equipped with Tiger I tanks, was the regiment's heavy company. This has led some researchers to interpret the S15, S17 and S25 turret numbers seen in contemporary photographs as indicating a Schwere-Kompanie but the letters almost certainly identify a tank of the battalion Stab, or headquarters.

At left: The Befehlspanzerwagen Panther ausf D of the battalion commander, Sturmbannführer Herbert Kuhlmann, numbered S15 was also photographed in northern Italy before the allocation of new tanks in November 1943. Compare the style of company number with that applied to the tank shown on the following page.

Tanks of 1.Kompanie lined up for inspection. Note that the company number is repeated on the turret rear. These vehicles were so mechanically unsound that it was decided that all would be returned and by the end of November 1943 a total of ninety-six new tanks were shipped from the Heereszeugamt. Although most sources state that these were all Panther ausf A models, photographic evidence shows that at least one Panther ausf D was in service with the battalion's 1.Kompanie and there may have been others. The numbering system was retained but the numbers and letters were now black with no outline. Sixty of the old tanks eventually found their way to Panzer-Abteilung (Panther/Bo.)Nord as explained in the text.

............*text continued from page 14*

Notes

1. The fighting at this time was centred on the area around the former Russian imperial palace of Oranienbaum which today has been absorbed by the St Petersburg suburb of Lomonosov. The term bodenständige signifies very limited mobility.

2. Two Bergepanther recovery tanks, which were promised by the Inspekteur der Panzertruppen, never arrived.

3. The date is given in an entry in the Kriegstagebuch, or war diary, of 4.SS-Panzergrenadier-Brigade Nederland which was temporarily attached to the division at the time.

Two hull-down positions were built for each tank and it was planned that ten Panthers be used as training vehicles, although in the event just three were available and these needed to be deployed close to the front.

On 23 November 1943, before the last vehicles had arrived, parts of I.Abteilung, Panzer-Regiment 29, which had been training in Germany and France since March, were transferred to Heeresgruppe Nord to man the static Panthers. Due to personnel losses the training of the Panzerjäger crews had not fulfilled expectations and although OKH now ordered that this be accelerated, on 29 November 1943 the commander of Heeresgruppe Nord requested that the men of Panzer-Regiment 29 remain at the front. Until they arrived the tanks were under the direct control of the Panzerjäger battalions of 9. and 10.Luftwaffen-Feld-Divisionen and each division operated a mobile reserve of five operational Panthers in addition to the static defences. Any maintenance was to be undertaken by the workshops of schwere Panzer-Abteilung 502, a Tiger battalion.

In early December, with the arrival of the Panzer-Regiment 29 crews, the Panthers were formed into bodenständige (bo) Panzer-Abteilung Oranienbaum (1) made up of a staff element and two companies of thirty Panthers each (2). The battalion was

subordinated to III.SS-Panzerkorps, which had recently been transferred from Croatia, on 12 December 1943 and four days later was renamed Panzer-Abteilung (Panther/Bo.) Nord. Most tanks were retained in their static positions but four operational vehicles took part in an attack on Christmas Eve in support of 4.SS-Polizei-Panzergrenadier-Division near Kernovo on the Voronka River, about 50 kilometres west of St Petersburg. A report compiled by III.SS-Panzerkorps dated 1 January 1944 states that fifty-two Panthers were on hand with I.Abteilung, Panzer-Regiment 29 of which thirty-one were capable of independent movement. These were distributed among the divisions and it is probable that the eight tanks that had supported 11.SS-Panzergrenadier-Division Nordland were taken over by that formation's Panzer battalion as early as 8 January 1944 and manned by Waffen-SS personnel (3).

Four days later the remaining operational Panthers of I.Abteilung, Panzer-Regiment 29 were officially handed over to SS-Panzer-Abteilung 11, bringing the total number to thirteen although a status report compiled in February mentions just five Panthers described as unbewegliche, or immobile. Incredibly, three of these tanks were still with the battalion in January 1945 and a veteran claims that the last Panther was destroyed in the fighting for Berlin.

This vehicle is one of the very early production Panther ausf D tanks allocated to SS-Panzer-Regiment 1, returned as unserviceable, and eventually operated by Panzer-Abteilung (Panther/Bo.) Nord. Note the first pattern drive sprocket, twin headlights and early cupola. This tank was later given a comprehensive coating of whitewash camouflage, which largely covered the number on the turret side, and is shown in the Camouflage & Markings section.

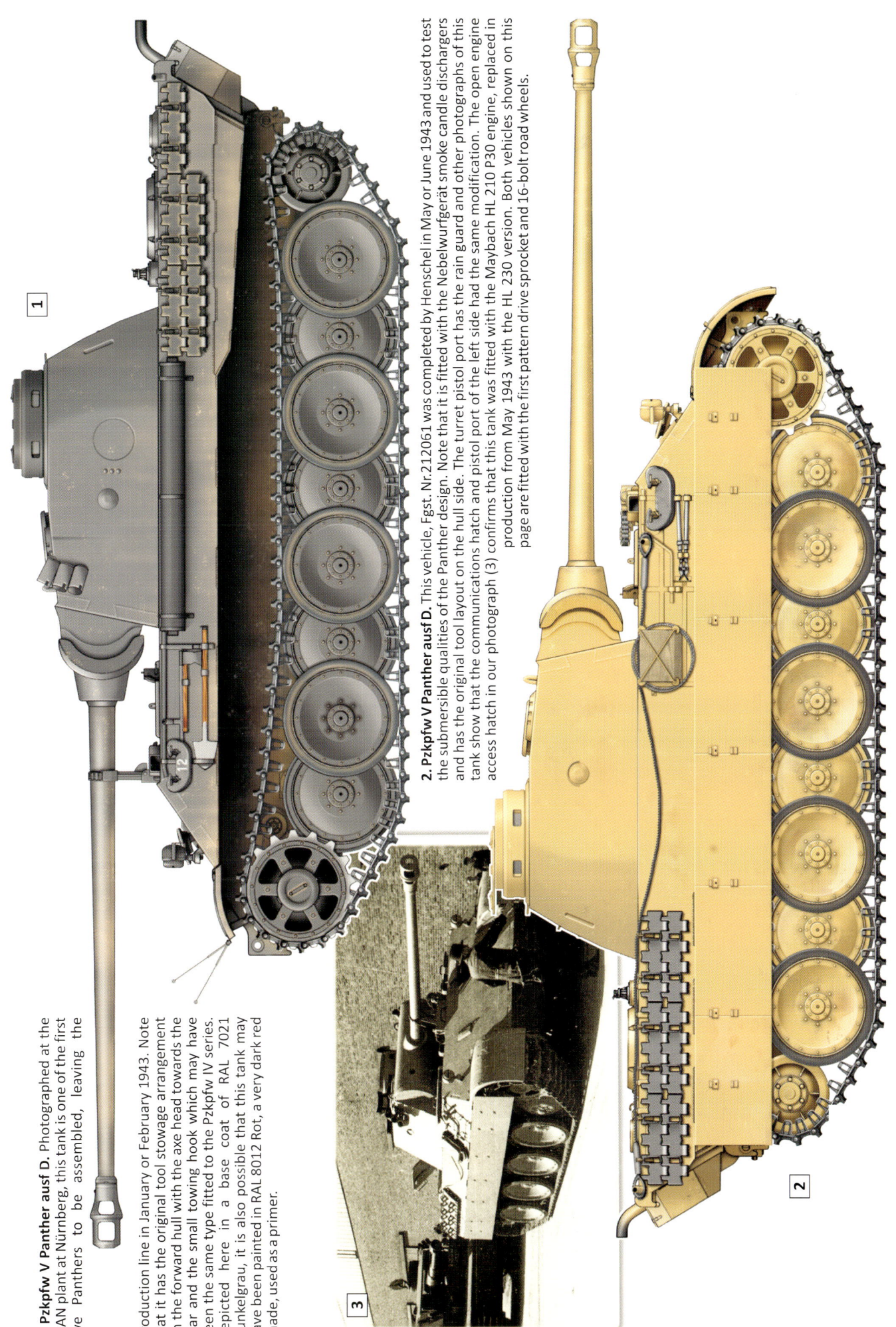

1. Pzkpfw V Panther ausf D. Photographed at the MAN plant at Nürnberg, this tank is one of the first five Panthers to be assembled, leaving the production line in January or February 1943. Note that it has the original tool stowage arrangement on the forward hull with the axe head towards the rear and the small towing hook which may have been the same type fitted to the Pzkpfw IV series. Depicted here in a base coat of RAL 7021 Dunkelgrau, it is also possible that this tank may have been painted in RAL 8012 Rot, a very dark red shade, used as a primer.

2. Pzkpfw V Panther ausf D. This vehicle, Fgst. Nr.212061 was completed by Henschel in May or June 1943 and used to test the submersible qualities of the Panther design. Note that it is fitted with the Nebelwurfgerät smoke candle dischargers and has the original tool layout on the hull side. The turret pistol port has the rain guard and other photographs of this tank show that the communications hatch and pistol port of the left side had the same modification. The open engine access hatch in our photograph (3) confirms that this tank was fitted with the Maybach HL 210 P30 engine, replaced in production from May 1943 with the HL 230 version. Both vehicles shown on this page are fitted with the first pattern drive sprocket and 16-bolt road wheels.

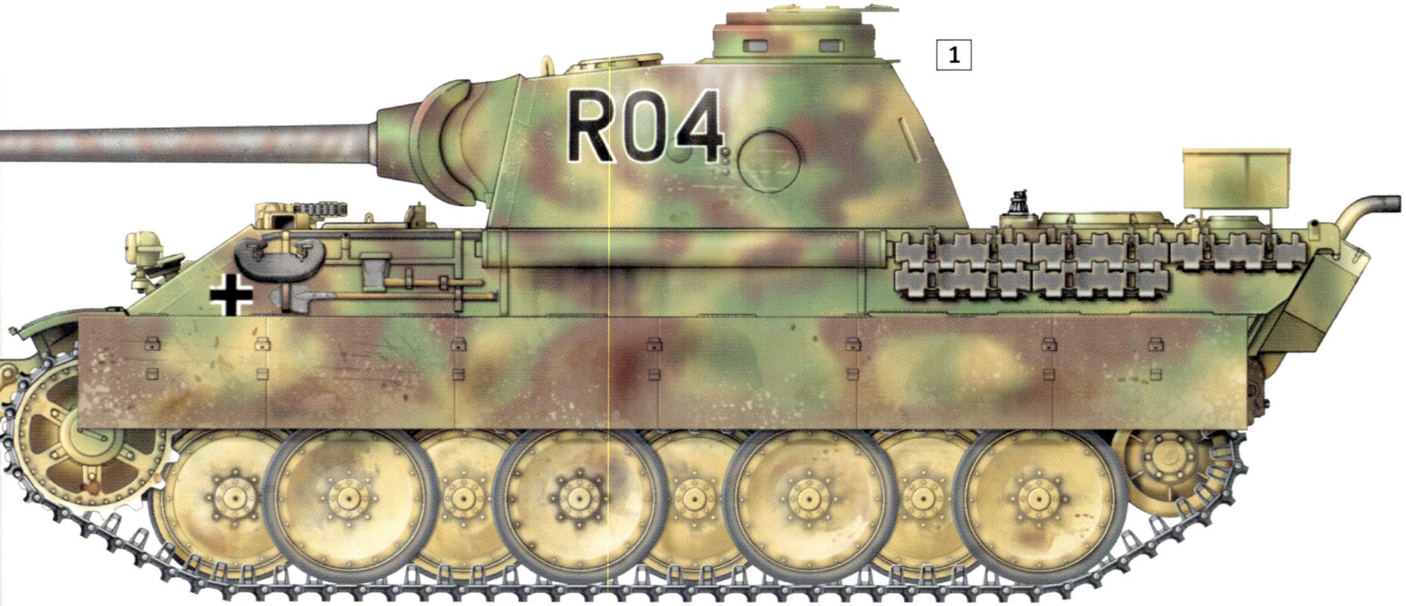

1. Pzkpfw V Panther ausf D. Stab, Panzer-Regiment von Lauchert. Western Russia, July 1943. This early production vehicle was fitted with two headlights, the second pattern drive sprocket and the rain channel over the turret communications hatch. Many tanks of this formation were modified to carry the wooden stowage boxes on the rear hull (2) and these could vary in size and shape. Replacement gun barrels were coated in a very dark heat-resistant lacquer and many were left unpainted or only lightly camouflaged. A photograph of this tank is reproduced on page 11.

3. Befehlspanzerwagen V Panther ausf D. Stab, Panzer-Abteilung 51. Western Russia, July 1943. Almost all the tanks of Panzer-Regiment von Lauchert were fitted with hull Schürzen and the supports which held the armour plates in place are shown here. Many vehicles were modified with the addition of a stowage locker on the hull side but these were far from universal and photographs show that some tanks had been fitted with the sledgehammer and track tensioning tool and on others the space was bare, as it was on very early production models. The boxes on the hull rear varied in size but all were mounted on metal frames that were welded over the air intake louvres. Note the armoured cover for the FuG 8 aerial insulator on the rear deck.

All the illustrations shown on this page are based on photographs of the Panthers of Panzer-Abteilung 51 taken during Operation Citadel.

1. Pzkpfw V Panther ausf D. 1.Kompanie, Panzer-Abteilung 51. The snarling Panther head insignia, almost universal among the tanks of Panzer-Abteilung 52, was rarely applied to the Panthers of this formation. The example shown here (2) is rendered in red, a colour which was commonly used to denote a first company. The marking is just visible on tank 124 (3) and is possibly the dark shape on the turret of tank 143 (4). But it is in all cases very unclear and our reconstruction should be regarded as speculative. The company number was repeated on the turret rear (5). Note the lack of smoke candle dischargers, unusual at this time.

6. Pzkpfw V Panther ausf D. 2.Kompanie, Panzer-Abteilung 51. This tank was an early production version with twin headlights, the second pattern drive sprocket, 16-bolt road wheels, large stowage locker on the hull right side and a full set of hull Schürzen. The company number was repeated on the turret rear (7) in a central position.

8. Pzkpfw V Panther ausf D. 3.Kompanie, Panzer-Abteilung 51. Photographed along the Oboyan road after the conclusion of the battles south of Kursk, this tank was one of thirty-one captured Panthers studied extensively by the Soviets. Fitted with twin headlights, it retained the front fender extensions which were incorporated at the assembly plant. The drive sprocket was the second pattern and the road wheels were the 16-bolt versions. A photograph of the right side has not survived but it was probably fitted with the large hull stowage locker. Note the bracket on the turret side towards the rear (9). The company number was repeated on the turret rear (10) and the Balkenkreuz (11) was applied between the exhaust mufflers, as was common at this time.

12. Pzkpfw V Panther ausf D. 4.Kompanie, Panzer-Abteilung 51. A number of sources claim that at least one tank of this company, Panther 434, carried the snarling panther badge in black on the turret side but I have been unable to find a single image which could confirm this. Unusually, the company number of the tank depicted here was rendered on the turret rear without a white outline (13) and this can be clearly seen in our photograph (14). But it is likely that most others had the white outline (15). A photograph of Panther 434 is reproduced on page 53.

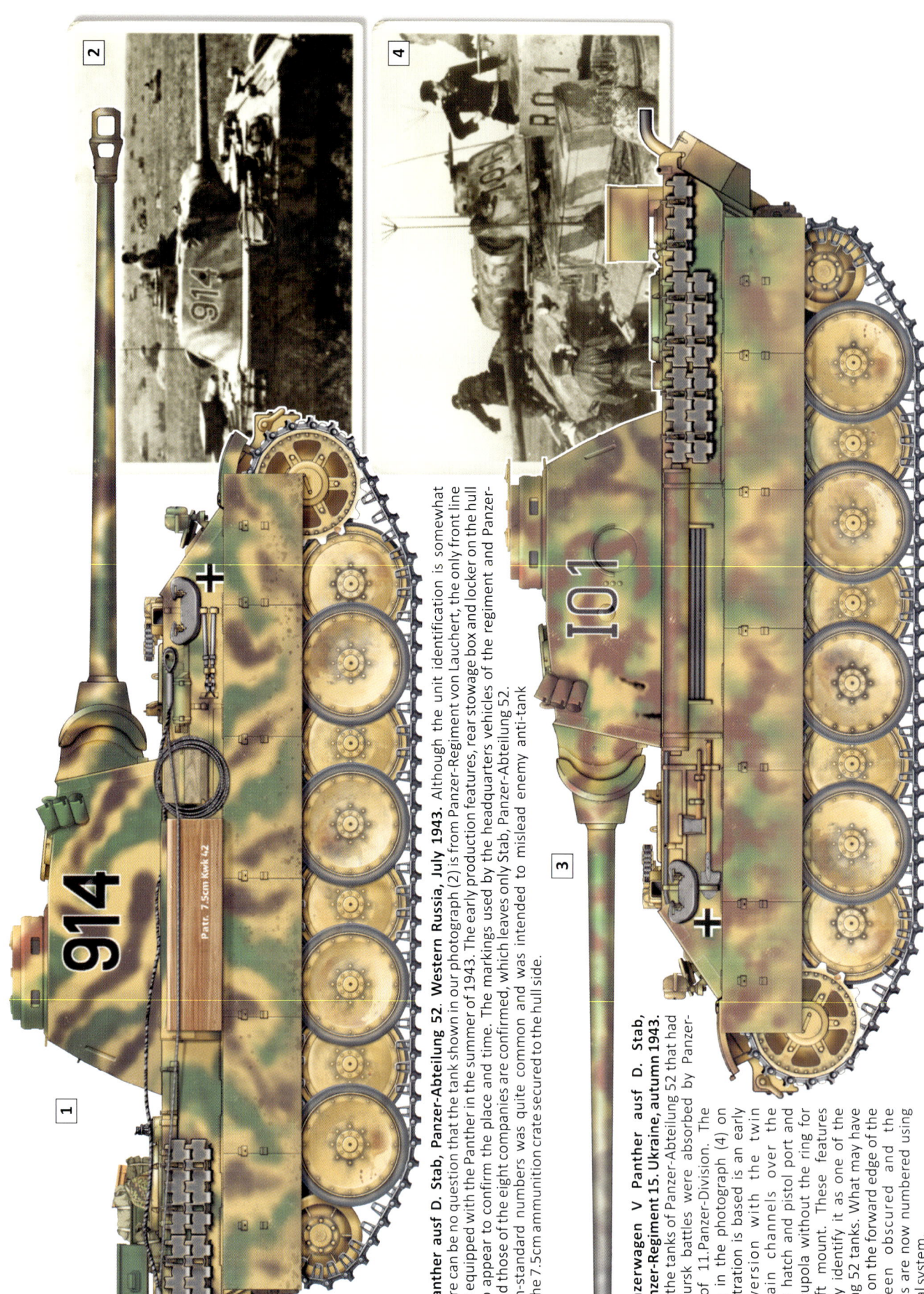

1. Pzkpfw V Panther ausf D. Stab, Panzer-Abteilung 52. Western Russia, July 1943. Although the unit identification is somewhat speculative there can be no question that the tank shown in our photograph (2) is from Panzer-Regiment von Lauchert, the only front line formation to be equipped with the Panther in the summer of 1943. The early production features, rear stowage box and locker on the hull side would also appear to confirm the place and time. The markings used by the headquarters vehicles of the regiment and Panzer-Abteilung 51 and those of the eight companies are confirmed, which leaves only Stab, Panzer-Abteilung 52. The use of non-standard numbers was quite common and was intended to mislead enemy anti-tank gunners. Note the 7.5cm ammunition crate secured to the hull side.

3. Befehlspanzerwagen V Panther ausf D. Stab, I.Abteilung, Panzer-Regiment 15. Ukraine, autumn 1943. In August 1943 the tanks of Panzer-Abteilung 52 that had survived the Kursk battles were absorbed by Panzer-Regiment 15 of 11.Panzer-Division. The Panther shown in the photograph (4) on which this illustration is based is an early production version with the twin headlights, rain channels over the communication hatch and pistol port and commander's cupola without the ring for the anti-aircraft mount. These features almost certainly identify it as one of the Panzer-Abteilung 52 tanks. What may have been a marking on the forward edge of the turret has been obscured and the battalion's tanks are now numbered using the conventional system.

All the illustrations shown on this page are based on photographs of the Panthers of Panzer-Abteilung 51 taken during Operation Citadel.

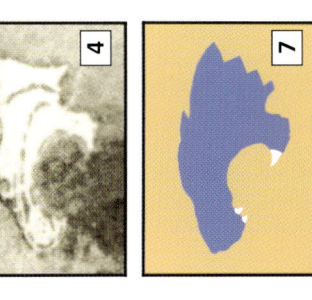
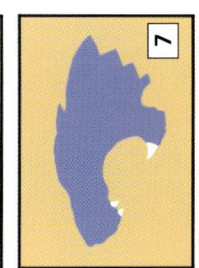
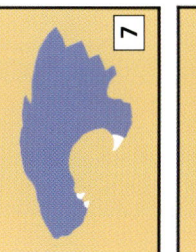

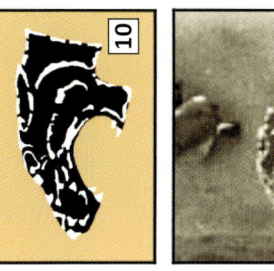
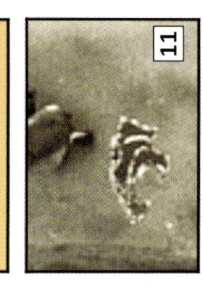
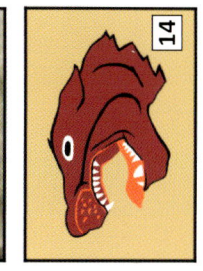
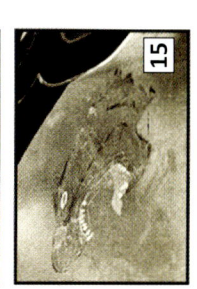

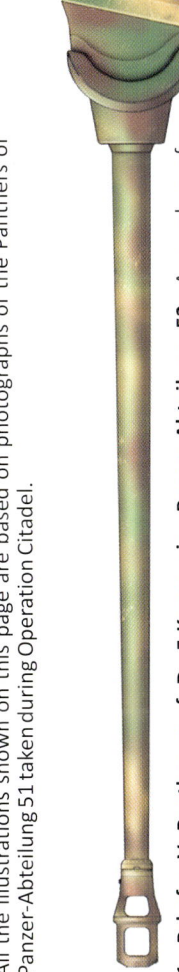

1. Pzkpfw V Panther ausf D. 5.Kompanie, Panzer-Abteilung 52. A number of photographs of this tank exist but most were taken after its capture and many features are missing. In addition, some markings may have been repainted at a later date. This tank was fitted with twin headlights, a binocular gun sight, the second pattern drive sprocket and a mix of 16-bolt and 24-bolt road wheels. The brackets which would have held the supports for the hull Schürzen were in place so we can assume that a full set of plates were originally fitted. The company number and panther insignia were repeated on the turret rear, although the number is approximately at half size (2). The panther badge (3) was rendered in white with black details as can be clearly seen from our photograph (4).

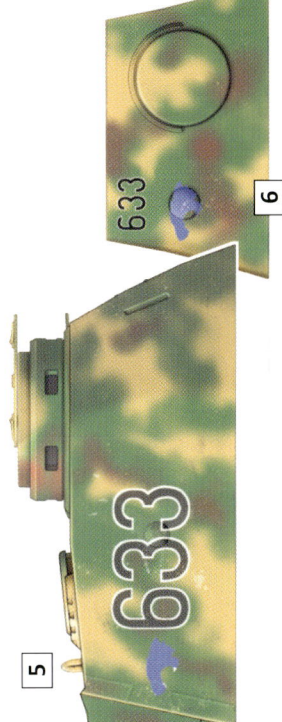

5. Pzkpfw V Panther ausf D. 6.Kompanie, Panzer-Abteilung 52. The tanks of this company are reported to have been identified by a snarling panther badge depicted in blue. Most sources suggest that this was a version of the 5.Kompanie insignia shown above but the only reliable image shows what appears to be a silhouette without detail. The placement of the unit insignia on the turret rear (6), over the pistol port, would seem to be somewhat inconvenient but is confirmed by photographs and was fairly consistent throughout the battalion. Note that the example on the turret side, just forward of the company number, appears to have white fangs (7). A photograph of this tank is reproduced on page 5.

8. Pzkpfw V Panther ausf D. 7.Kompanie, Panzer-Abteilung 51. Photographed during the early stages of Operation Citadel this tank was fitted with wooden stowage boxes on the hull rear, twin headlights, the binocular gun sight, the second pattern drive sprocket and a mix of 16-bolt and 24-bolt road wheels. The company number and panther badge were painted onto the turret side and also the rear (9). The unit insignia is almost identical to that seen on the tanks of 5.Kompanie but the colours are reversed (10) as can be seen by our photograph (11) of Panther 745.

12. Pzkpfw V Panther ausf D. 8.Kompanie, Panzer-Abteilung 51. Captured almost intact, this tank is shown in numerous photographs throughout this book. As with the other vehicles of the battalion, the company number and unit insignia were carried on the turret side and possibly the rear although the panther badge is missing from this tank (13). The design of the badge itself (14) is markedly different from those employed by the other companies and is quite obviously hand painted. The colours used here are conjectural, although highly likely, but the details are accurate as can be seen from our photograph (15).

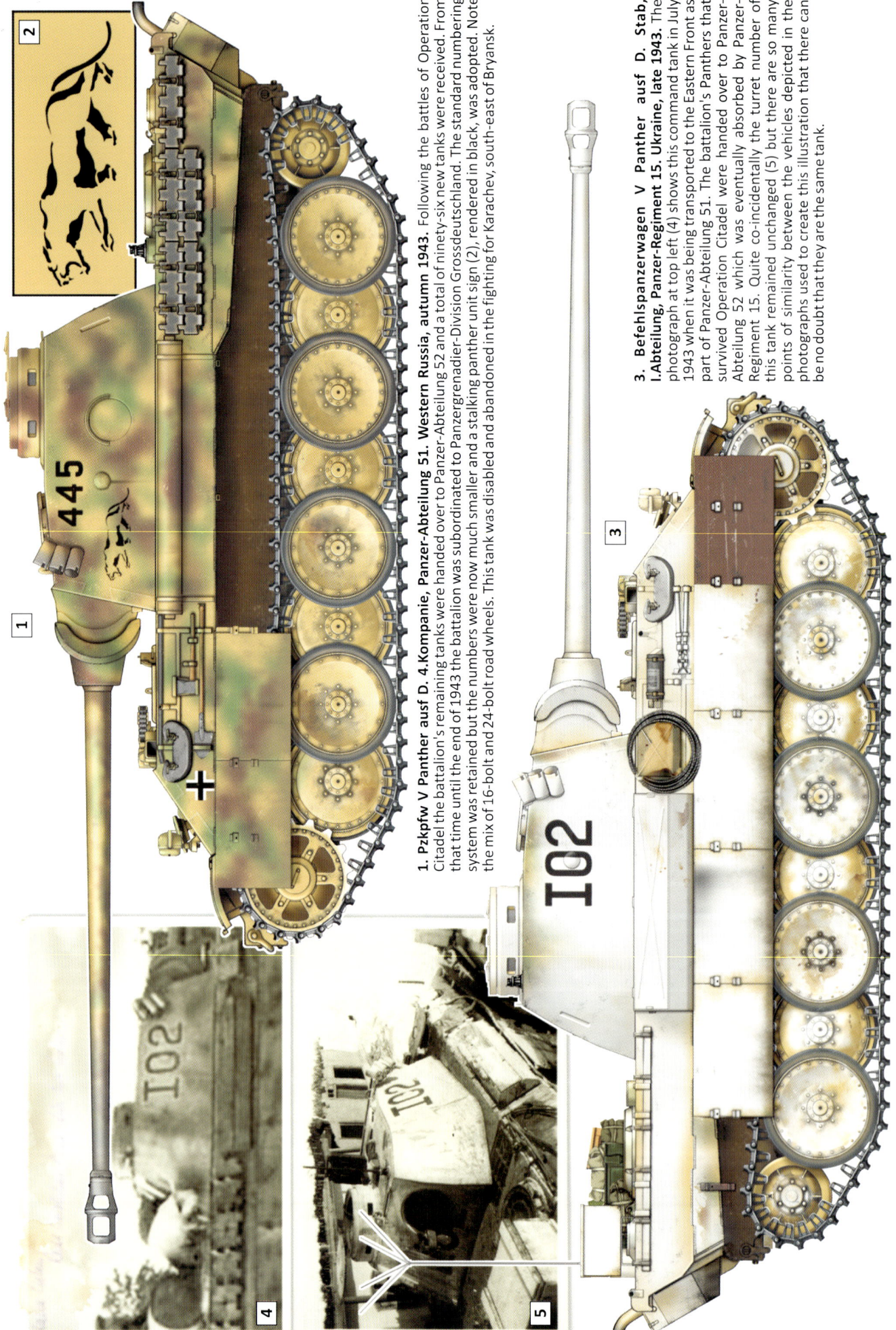

1. Pzkpfw V Panther ausf D. 4.Kompanie, Panzer-Abteilung 51. Western Russia, autumn 1943. Following the battles of Operation Citadel the battalion's remaining tanks were handed over to Panzer-Abteilung 52 and a total of ninety-six new tanks were received. From that time until the end of 1943 the battalion was subordinated to Panzergrenadier-Division Grossdeutschland. The standard numbering system was retained but the numbers were now much smaller and a stalking panther unit sign (2), rendered in black, was adopted. Note the mix of 16-bolt and 24-bolt road wheels. This tank was disabled and abandoned in the fighting for Karachev, south-east of Bryansk.

3. Befehlspanzerwagen V Panther ausf D. Stab, I.Abteilung, Panzer-Regiment 15. Ukraine, late 1943. The photograph at top left (4) shows this command tank in July 1943 when it was being transported to the Eastern Front as part of Panzer-Abteilung 51. The battalion's Panthers that survived Operation Citadel were handed over to Panzer-Abteilung 52 which were eventually absorbed by Panzer-Regiment 15. Quite co-incidentally the turret number of this tank remained unchanged (5) but there are so many points of similarity between the vehicles depicted in the photographs used to create this illustration that there can be no doubt that they are the same tank.

1

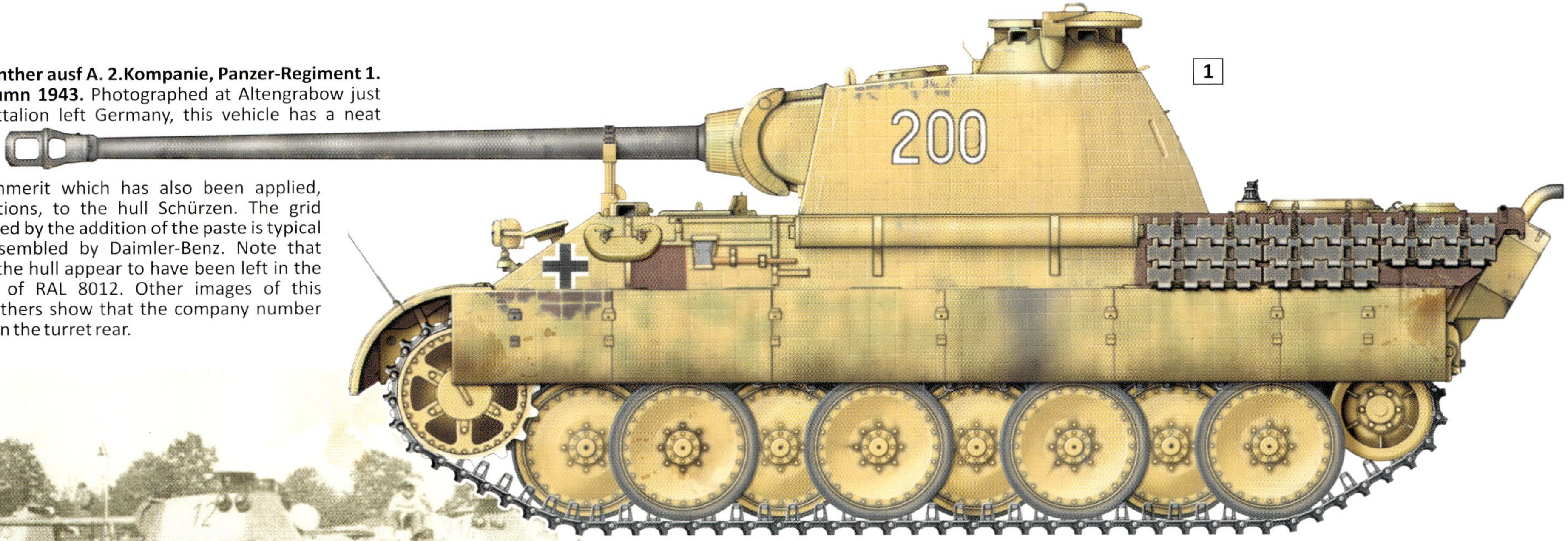

1. Pzkpfw V Panther ausf A. 2.Kompanie, Panzer-Regiment 1. Germany, autumn 1943. Photographed at Altengrabow just before the battalion left Germany, this vehicle has a neat coating of Zimmerit which has also been applied, against regulations, to the hull Schürzen. The grid pattern produced by the addition of the paste is typical of vehicles assembled by Daimler-Benz. Note that some parts of the hull appear to have been left in the primer colour of RAL 8012. Other images of this battalion's Panthers show that the company number was repeated on the turret rear.

2

3

2. Befehlspanzerwagen V Panther ausf D. Stab, I.Abteilung, Panzer-Regiment 2. Germany, autumn 1943. Based on the worn snapshot shown at left (3), it is not possible to determine if this tank was coated with Zimmerit as is claimed in some sources. The hand-written notation on the reverse of our photograph reads: *'PR 2 Verladung der I Abteilung in Grafenwöhr September 1943'*. As the battalion's tanks were all shipped from the Heereszeugamt by 11 September, it is likely that very few received an application of the anti-magnetic mine paste at the assembly plants. Note the metal bracket that supports the cupola hatch.

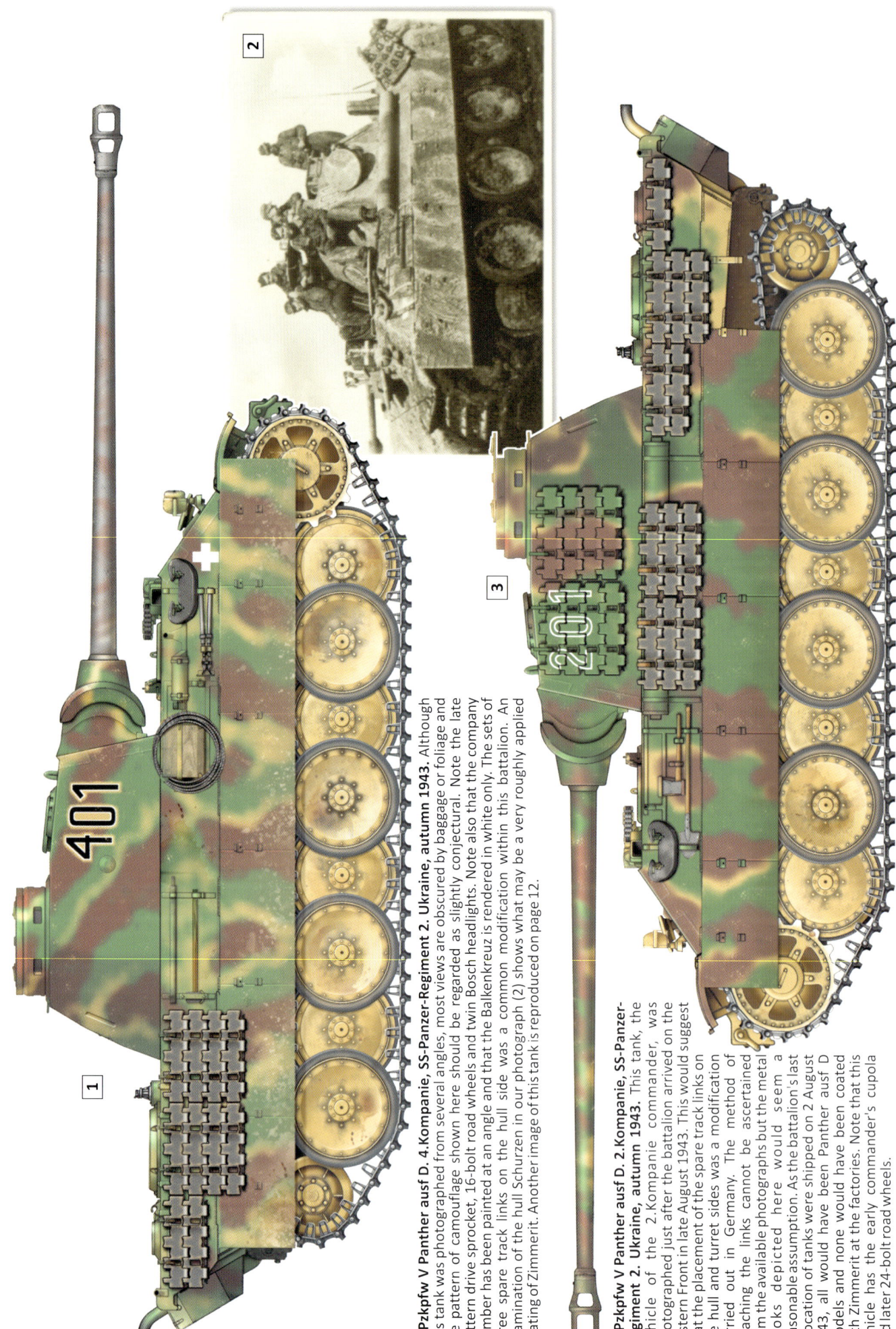

1. Pzkpfw V Panther ausf D. 4.Kompanie, SS-Panzer-Regiment 2. Ukraine, autumn 1943. Although this tank was photographed from several angles, most views are obscured by baggage or foliage and the pattern of camouflage shown here should be regarded as slightly conjectural. Note the late pattern drive sprocket, 16-bolt road wheels and twin Bosch headlights. Note also that the company number has been painted at an angle and that the Balkenkreuz is rendered in white only. The sets of three spare track links on the hull side was a common modification within this battalion. An examination of the hull Schurzen in our photograph (2) shows what may be a very roughly applied coating of Zimmerit. Another image of this tank is reproduced on page 12.

3. Pzkpfw V Panther ausf D. 2.Kompanie, SS-Panzer-Regiment 2. Ukraine, autumn 1943. This tank, the vehicle of the 2.Kompanie commander, was photographed just after the battalion arrived on the Eastern Front in late August 1943. This would suggest that the placement of the spare track links on the hull and turret sides was a modification carried out in Germany. The method of attaching the links cannot be ascertained from the available photographs but the metal hooks depicted here would seem a reasonable assumption. As the battalion's last allocation of tanks were shipped on 2 August 1943, all would have been Panther ausf D models and none would have been coated with Zimmerit at the factories. Note that this vehicle has the early commander's cupola and later 24-bolt road wheels.

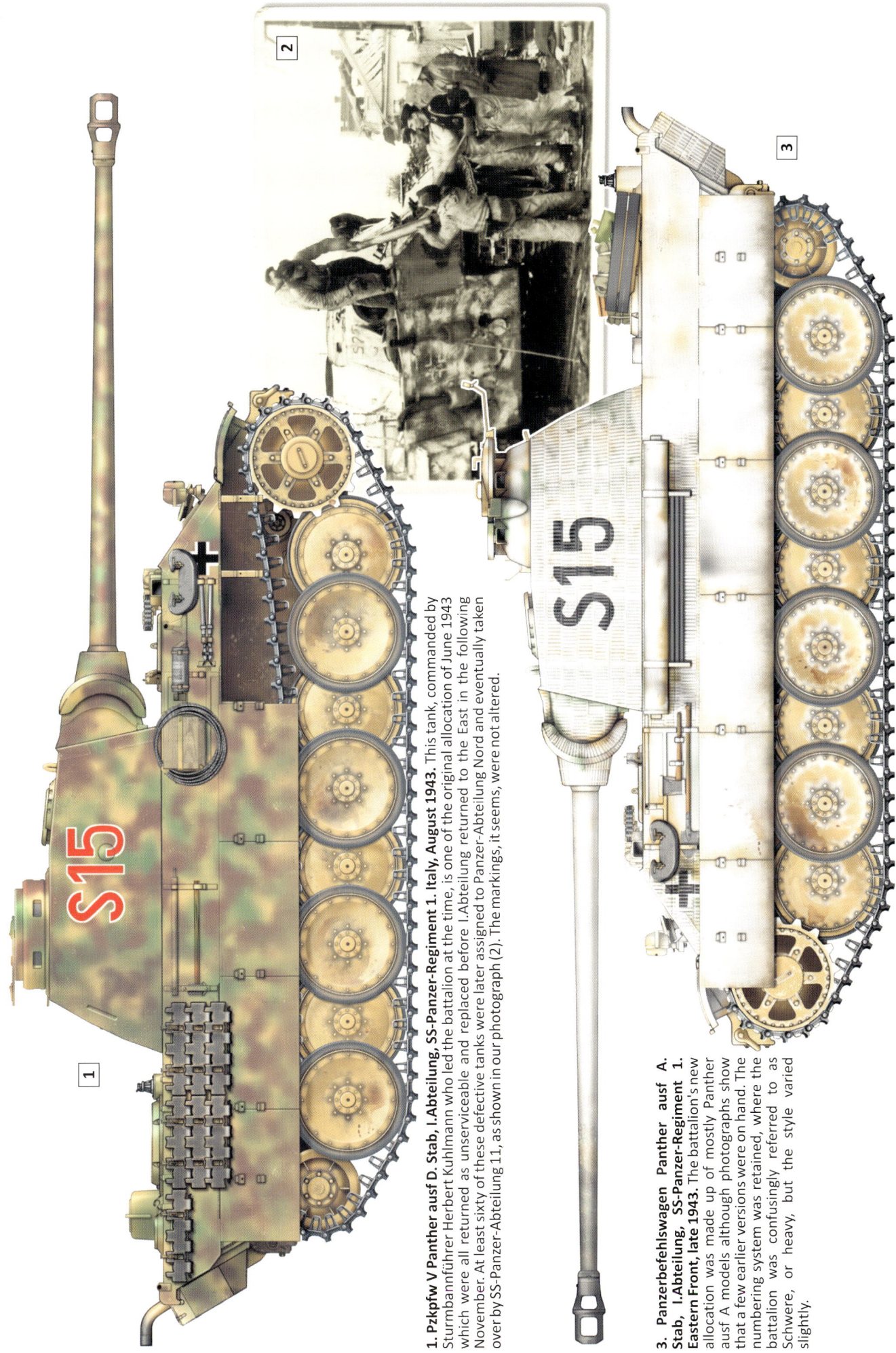

1. Pzkpfw V Panther ausf D. Stab, I.Abteilung, SS-Panzer-Regiment 1. Italy, August 1943. This tank, commanded by Sturmbannführer Herbert Kuhlmann who led the battalion at the time, is one of the original allocation of June 1943 which were all returned as unserviceable and replaced before I.Abteilung returned to the East in the following November. At least sixty of these defective tanks were later assigned to Panzer-Abteilung Nord and eventually taken over by SS-Panzer-Abteilung 11, as shown in our photograph (2). The markings, it seems, were not altered.

3. Panzerbefehlswagen Panther ausf A. Stab, I.Abteilung, SS-Panzer-Regiment 1. Eastern Front, late 1943. The battalion's new allocation was made up of mostly Panther ausf A models although photographs show that a few earlier versions were on hand. The numbering system was retained, where the battalion was confusingly referred to as Schwere, or heavy, but the style varied slightly.

1. Pzkpfw V Panther ausf A. Unidentified unit. Eastern Front, late 1943.
Although this tank, Fgst Nr.151951, was assembled by Daimler-Benz in the first days of October 1943 it does not have a coating of Zimmerit which would seem to confirm that some manufacturers had difficulty sourcing the paste. Although not visible here, this tank was fitted with twin apertures for the binocular gun sight and wide rain channel. Note that the ring for the cupola anti-aircraft machine-gun mount is missing.

2. Pzkpfw V Panther ausf A. 7.Kompanie, Panzer-Regiment 23. Eastern Front, late 1943. This tank provides another example of a September or October 1943 production vehicle which did not receive a coating of Zimmerit before leaving the assembly plant. Our photograph (3) shows the unusual application of whitewash camouflage were a large part of the hull glacis and main gun manlet have been left in the original colours.

PANTHER AUSF D
SS-PANZER-REGIMENT 2
THEODOROS KALAMATAS
1/35 SCALE

Regular readers of this series will be familiar with the high-quality models built and painted by Theodoros. This replica of a Panther ausf D was based on the Zvezda kit in 1/35 scale. Theodoros found the model to be accurate, detailed and easy to assemble and added only photo-etched brass screens to the engine rear deck.

The tracks are supplied as individual links and are fully workable. The completed model was finished in Tamyia acrylics and weathered with pigments from Ammo by MIG and AK Interactive.

The figures are from a Tamiya kit and were painted in artists oils for the flesh and Vallejo acrylics for the camouflage overalls.

PANTHER AUSF D
PANZER-ABTEILUNG 52
KENTARO TAKABAYASHI
1/35 SCALE

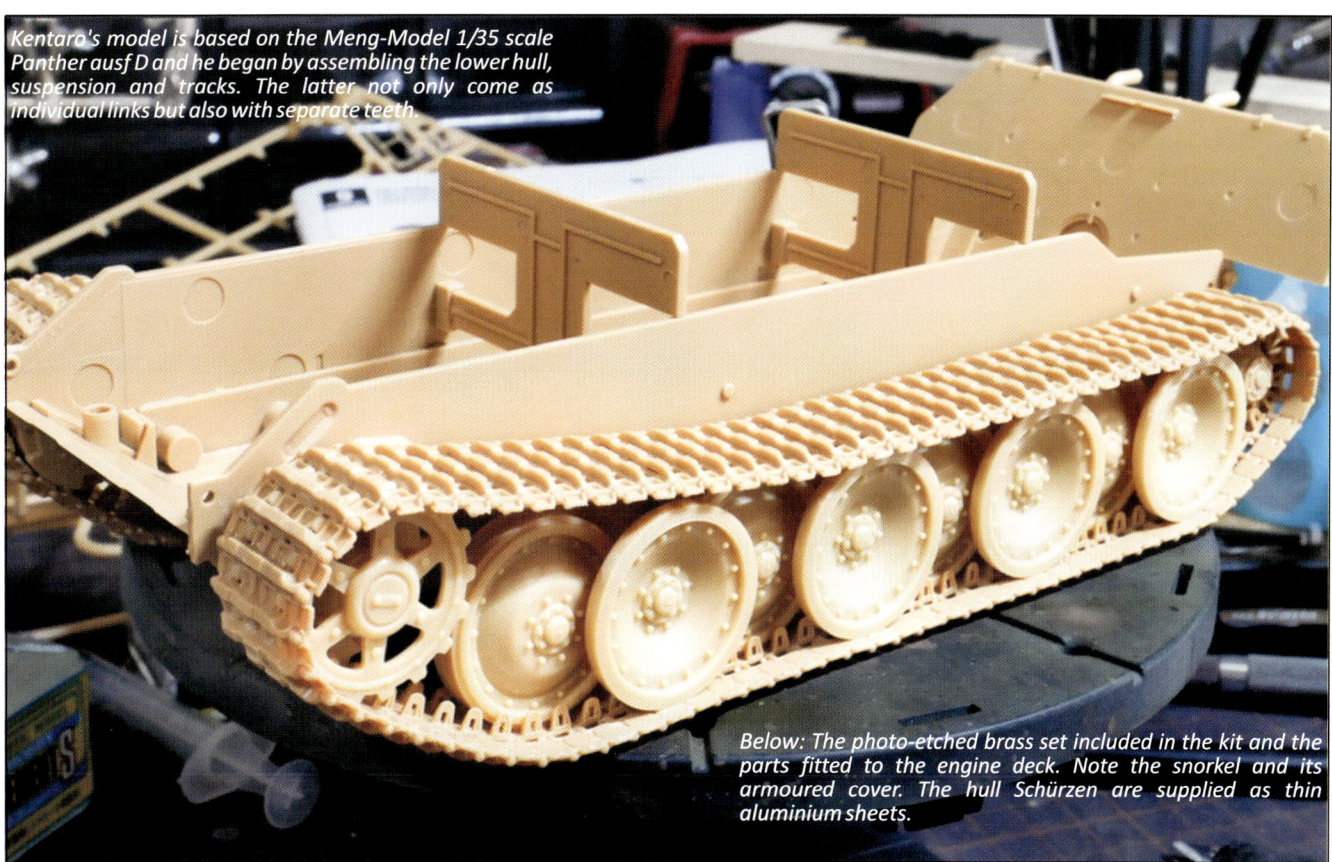

Kentaro's model is based on the Meng-Model 1/35 scale Panther ausf D and he began by assembling the lower hull, suspension and tracks. The latter not only come as individual links but also with separate teeth.

Below: The photo-etched brass set included in the kit and the parts fitted to the engine deck. Note the snorkel and its armoured cover. The hull Schürzen are supplied as thin aluminium sheets.

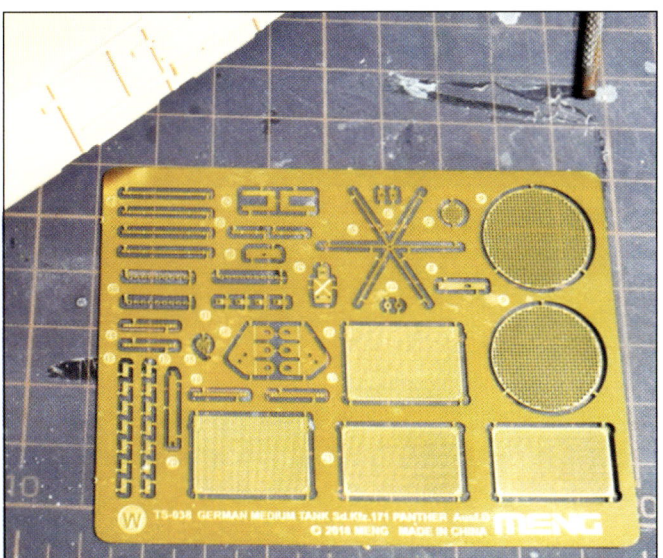

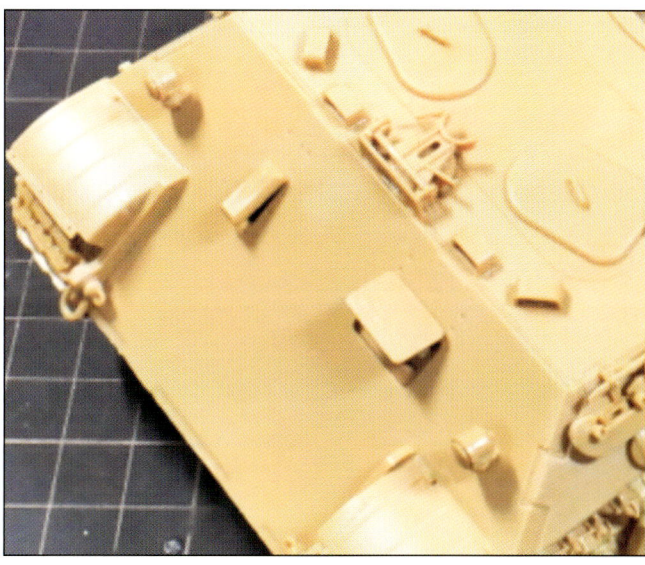

The fully assembled model with the snorkel extended. The stowage boxes on the hull rear were an identifying feature of the tanks which took part in Operation Citadel. The metal hatch cover for the commander's cupola is supplied with the kit.

The first coat of camouflage colours applied using Tamiya acrylics.

At right: A view of the completed model. The markings are those supplied with the kit and were applied using Mr. Mark Softener and Coolsmile Racing Decal Fitter No.1, both popular with Japanese modellers. Below: Details of the finished model including the commander's cupola. Kentaro realised that this tank was not fitted withn the anti-aircraft ring in July 1943 but speculated that it may have been added by the autumn. The smoke candel dischargers are fully loaded and the snorkel is in place. Note the fire extinguisher in its bracket on the tool rack. Made by the firm of Tetra, these were often left unpainted, as shown here.

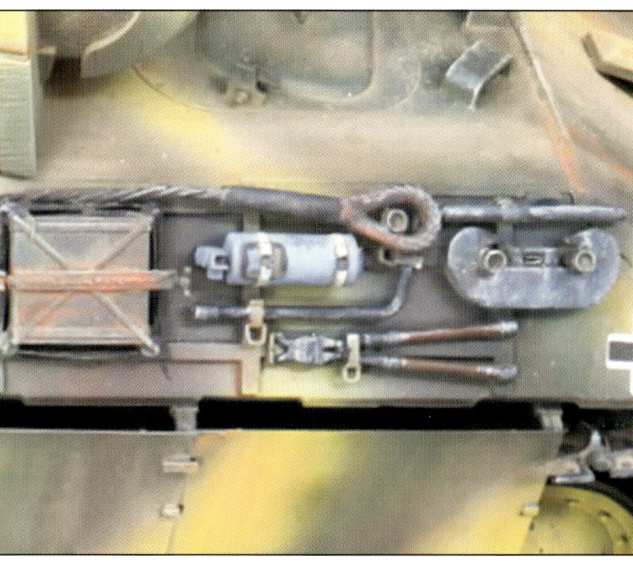

Another view of the finished model showing the arrangement of the right side tool rack and the early bracket for the wooden jack block.

A rear view of Kentaro's completed model showing the wooden stowage boxes, early exhaust mufflers and horizontally positioned jack. Note the armoured cover for the FuG 8 command radio aerial insulator behind the snorkel.

PANTHER AUSF A
EASTERN FRONT
SEBASTIAN KEUDELL
1/35 SCALE

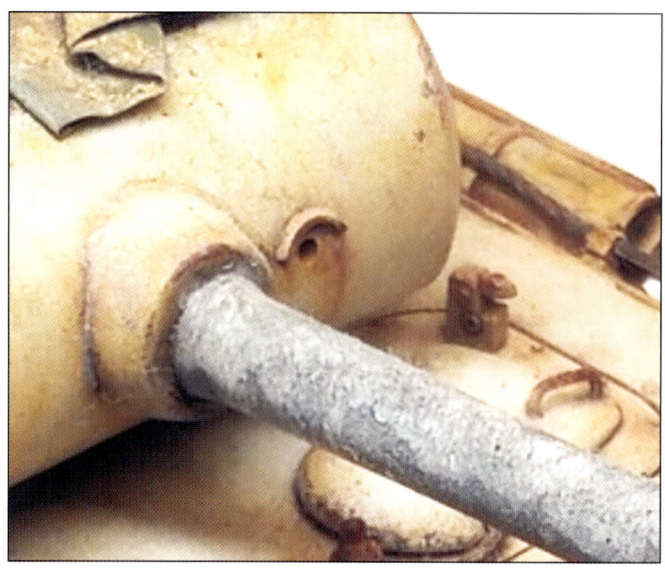

Argentinian modeller Sebastian Keudell's replica is based on the Italeri 1/35 scale kit. Representing a Panther ausf A assembled after November 1943, when the Kugelblende machine-gun mount was introduced into production, this tank does not have a coating of Zimmerit. Although it was introduced in September 1943, a number of manufacturers experienced difficulty in procuring sufficient quantities of the anti-magnetic mine paste and units in the field were not directed to apply Zimmerit until the following November. In addition, Panthers photographed at the MAN plant in January 1944 suggest that tanks were still leaving the assembly lines without a coat of Zimmerit.

Further views of Sebastian's completed model showing the engine louvre protective grills and the Maybach HL230 P30 engine. The cast commander's cupola, the main identifying feature of the Panther ausf A, was considerably easier and cheaper to produce than the earlier so-called drum style. The worn whitewash camouflage is quite realistic and should be compared to the photographs on pages 22 and 26.

PANTHER AUSF D

PANZER-ABTEILUNG 51

SUNGJUN JANG

1/48 SCALE

Prolific Korean modeller Sungjun used the Tamiya 1/48 scale kit as the basis for his replica. Shown above, built and ready to paint, it was assembled almost straight from the box with the addition of scratch-built engine louvre grills. Shown below is the completed model with one of the huge selection of adhesives, pigments and weathering products from the Ammo range produced by Mig Jimenez.

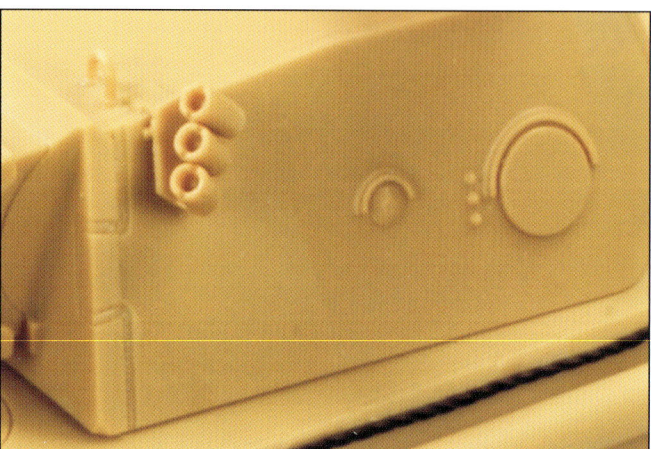

Above: Details of the built model including the commander figure, early style drive sprocket and track, engine deck and smoke candle dischargers.
Below: Sungjun's completed model after extensive weathering.

Above: The completed model in the markings of 4.Kompanie, Panzer-Abteilung 51. Note the wire grills on the engine deck. These were scratchbuilt by Sungjun and are the only parts that did not come with the kit. At right: A close up view of the mud-encrusted tracks, drive sprocket and 16-bolt wheels.

Below: Another view of the completed model. Note how the company number is place over the side pistol port. Very few 4.Kompanie tanks carried the panther head insignia, and it is quite correctly missing here, but one example can be seen on page 64.

As one of the most famous armoured fighting vehicles produced during the Second World War it should come as no surprise that model replicas of the Panther tank are currently available in sizes ranging from 1/285 scale wargames tanks to massive 1/6 scale radio-controlled vehicles. Unfortunately there are far too many to list here individually and, as with the other books in this series, I have chosen to concentrate on the most popular modelling scales of 1/35 and 1/48. As many of the currently available kits and accessories are covered in *Panther Tanks: German Army and Waffen-SS Normandy Campaign, 1944, Panther Tanks: German Army and Waffen-SS Defence of the West, 1945, Panther Tanks: German Army Panzer Brigades Western and Eastern Fronts, 1944-1945* and *Panther Medium Tank: IV.SS-Panzerkorps Eastern Front, 1944* I have chosen to expand the Model Showcase section of this book and reduce the number of pages that would normally make up this chapter. In addition I have tried to include those products which would have a bearing on the tanks that entered service between summer 1943 and the end of that year. As always, an index of manufacturers, with their contact details, can be found on page 64. Finally, the reader should note that for this chapter, as in the previous books, I have used the word Type in place of the more correct Ausführung, as at least one major manufacturer does, solely to avoid confusion.

DRAGON MODELS

Dragon Models was one of the first of the major manufacturers to offer accurate replicas in 1/35 scale and their kits are today something of a benchmark. The company's small scale releases are some of the best available. Since 2002 Dragon has released four models of the Panther Type D, including a version with Zimmerit and a model of the V2 prototype. The first kit to be released could be built as either a vehicle of Panzer-Abteilung 52 which served in the Kursk battles or Panzer-Abteilung 51 in late 1943. This model was re-released in 2020 with new parts. An early production Panther Type A was also released in 2002 and it should be note that although the vehicle depicted on the box has a coating of Zimmerit, the pattern typical of Daimler-Benz produced vehicles, this is not included in the kit. Dragon's 1/72 scale Panther Type D kit was completely re-worked and re-released in 2020 and is almost certainly the best replica in this scale.

At left: Dragon Models' Panther Type A early production kit in 1/72 scale with artwork by the great Ron Volstad. Note that the actual model does not have Zimmerit texture and it is actually a later production Panther Type D.

At right: Dragon's Panther Type D kit in 1/35 scale built with the photo-etched brass upgrade set from E.T. Model. Below: Details of the Dragon Models' late production Panther Type D model in 1/35 scale.

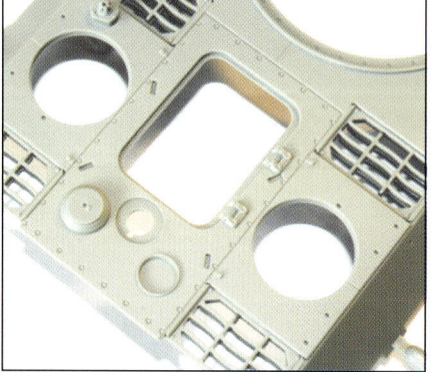

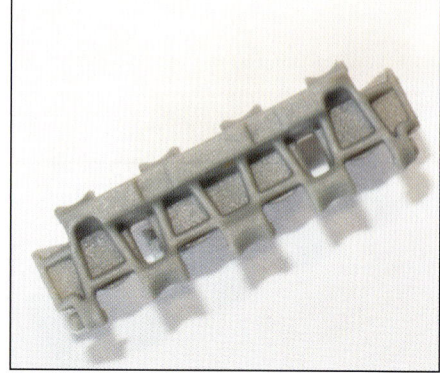

TAMIYA INCORPORATED

Since the early 1970s Tamiya has been producing a large range of armoured vehicles and was almost solely responsible for the rise in popularity of 1/35 scale. The company's Panther Type D was released in 2015 and again in 2018 as a special edition model which contains photo-etched brass details, a metal gun barrel, individual workable track links and increased marking options. Somewhat confusingly, it appears that recent examples of the earlier kit contain some or all of the special edition extras. Tamiya's Panther Type A kit was first released in 1990 and has not been changed since that time and lacks the detail of the company's newer releases. In 2019 Tamiya released a 1/48 scale Panther Type D which in many respects is a scaled down, albeit slightly simplified, version of the larger kit.

Above: Tamiya kits have always been accompanied by outstanding box art, which at times has run to the dramatic. The 1/35 scale Panther Type A shown above has changed little since it was first released.

At right: Tamiya's 1/48 scale Panther Type D built and painted according to the kit's instructions. Below: Details of the 1/48 scale model shown at right including the first pattern drive sprocket, turret, exhaust mufflers and jack.

TRUMPETER/HOBBY BOSS

Often thought to be separate entities, these Chinese companies are in fact owned by the same corporation, are located at the same address and are essentially the same firm although different models are marketed separately under the two labels. In 2021 Trumpeter announced future projects in 1/72 scale of a Panther Type D and Panther Type A. No details are available on exactly what these kits may include or when they will be released. Under the Hobby Boss label the company produces an early production Panther Type A with optional Zimmerit in 1/35 scale.

The Trumpeter/Hobby Boss Panther Type A in 1/35 scale built with the photo-etched brass upgrade set from Tetra Models. Zimmerit is supplied with the kit, in a pattern very similar to that seen on DEMAG-assembled vehicles, in the shape of fifty-one thin plastic sheets.

ICM

This Ukrainian company offers an extensive range of model kits including aircraft, ships, figures and armoured vehicles. Some unusual subjects are covered, such as the 1/35 scale 7.5cm Marder I Panzerjäger based on the French FCM tank chassis and an Sdkfz 247 command vehicle. The company's Panther Type D was first released in 2005 and was a completely new kit, contrary to what has been stated elsewhere. The model has also been re-boxed by Revell as a Panther Type D and Bergepanther, and in 2018 by Russian company Modelist. ICM also offers an early and late version of the Bergepanther recovery tank and both are based on the Panther Type D offering.

MENG-MODEL

Although based on the company's 2017 Panther Type A, the recently released Panther Type D contains many new parts. The kit includes photo-etched brass details, a metal gun barrel, separate sheets of Zimmerit texture and extensive marking options, all but one for the period covered by this book. There are also optional parts for a Befehlspanzerwagen command tank. The Special Release Panther Type D, catalogue no.ES-003, perpetuates the myth that Ernst Barkmann was the commander of Panther 401 in late 1943 but perhaps this should not detract from the quality of these kits. The box of the Panther Type D also carries the logo of the Bovington Tank Museum, implying their cooperation, although I have been unable to confirm this.

Above: Meng-Model's Panther Type D kit and the recently announced early production Panther Type A model. At right: The Panther Type D complete with snorkel and stowage boxes mounted on the engine deck.

Below: Details of the model shown at right including the main gun travel lock, the snorkel and armoured cover for the submersible equipment with stowage boxes and the left side tool rack.

ITALERI

First released in 1993, the company's Panther Type D model has been re-boxed several times, notably by Revell, Heller, Zvezda and the World of Tanks franchise. The latest Italeri offering has been reworked and contains photo-etched parts and markings for two late 1943 vehicles. The Panther Type A kit utilises many of the parts from the earlier kit with the option of Zimmerit texture which is supplied as thin plastic sheets. Of the large model manufacturers Italeri alone has ventured into 1/56 scale with a post-November 1943 production Panther Type A kit. This scale complements 28mm wargames figures of which there are now quite a number on the market.

At left: Italeri's 1/56 scale Panther Type A. Aimed primarily at the wargaming market, this model represents a tank assembled at the very end of the period covered by this book. Below: The Italeri 1/35 scale Type D kit partly completed with the upgrade set from Voyager model.

REVELL

Like Airfix, this company has gone through many changes of ownership over the years since its founding in 1943, at one time operating as two distinct entities in the US and Germany. The first in the series of 1/72 scale Panthers, details of which are shown below, were released in 1996 and were at that time the best small scale armoured vehicles available. Later releases from other firms, such as Dragon, did much to show up the inaccuracies in both the Panther Type A and Panther Type D but they were far ahead of their contemporaries. The 1/35 scale Panther Type A kit, released in 1997 and still available, is a re-boxing of the Italeri model with new markings.

TAKOM

One of the newest model manufacturers, this company started operating in Hong Kong in 2013 as Takom World and shortly afterwards expanded to open a plant in mainland China where all the models are now produced. First released in 2018, the company's Panther type D features a full interior and bonus transparent shell for the turret and hull. The same vehicle, with different marking options, is also offered as a later production tank. Both the Takom Panther Type A and Panther Type D were re-boxed in 2019 and sold under the Das Werk label, which is owned by Modellbaukönig, a German firm. As far as I have been able to ascertain these are the Takom kits without the interior details.

At left: Not to be outdone by Suyata (see next page) Takom has announced the future release of a 1/35 scale 16t Strabokran and Panther Type A.

Above: The 1/35 scale early production Panther Type A from Das Werk. This is in fact the Takom kit without the extensive interior details.

At left: Part of the interior of Takom's early production Panther Type A model. Above: The 1/35 scale Panther Type D kit built with full interior and optional transparent hull and turret.

ZVEZDA

The company's 1/35 scale Panther Type D was originally released in 2014 with markings for two Panzer-Abteilung 52 tanks and is based on the Italeri kit which was first marketed in 1993. Zvezda's Panther Type D in 1/72 scale is somewhat basic and while it is extremely good value for the price it cannot be compared to the Dragon offerings. The 1/100 scale Panther Type D is a rather simple snap-together model and is compatible with 15mm wargames figures.

Zvezda's Panther Type D built with the photo-etched brass detail set from Tetra Modelworks.

SUYATA

This Chinese company is a relative newcomer and is known more for its unusual, if not quirky, model subjects. The company's first armour release was the spectacular 1/48 scale diorama featuring a Panther Type A and huge 16t Strabokran crane complete with base. The tank is highly detailed and contains many interior parts but it should be mentioned that it can only be built as a post-November 1943 production variant with the Kugelblende machine-gun mount.

At right: Suyata's 16t Strabokran with Panther Type A and diorama base. Above: Details of the turret rear and the engine deck of the Panther Type A. Note that the Zimmerit texture comes as an optional extra.

In May 1942 orders for the first production tanks were placed with Maschinenfabrik Augsburg-Nürnberg (MAN), Daimler-Benz (DB), Maschinenfabrik Niedersachsen Hannover (MNH) and Henschel und Sohn. All these firms assembled complete vehicles except Henschel which received the turrets from Wegmann & Co at Kassel which were then mounted on a finished chassis at Henschel's assembly plant a short distance away. The company had also employed this arrangement with the production of the Tiger I. From the original order for 1,000 tanks, later reduced to 850, a total of twelve chassis were used as the first Bergepanther recovery vehicles.

When production first commenced in January 1943 the tanks were referred to as Pzkpfw Panther (7.5cm KwK 42 L/70) (Sd.Kfz.17) but the term Panther I is also known to have been used at around the same time, obviously to distinguish the design from the Panther II. The latter was under development and it was hoped, together with the Tiger II, that it would replace the earlier models.

The term Panther 1 ausf D (1) appears to have been used as early as April 1943 and is definitely included in a report compiled in the following November which compares the tank's armour with that of the Panther II. By May 1943 it was obvious that the Panther II project would be shelved and therefore production of the Panther I, which had until that time been regarded as an interim solution, was to continue. By July 1943, the next model in the Panther I

series, which would incorporate the improvements made to the first tanks and a number of new features, was being referred to as Pzkpfw Panther ausf A. I can offer no explanation as to why this designation was chosen or why the final version was named Pzkpfw Panther ausf G and although any number of theories have been put forward as to why these letters were used there is no definitive proof to support any (2). Purely as a matter of convenience I have used the terms Panther ausf D and Panther ausf A throughout this book to described the first and second production series respectively.

The Panther ausf A model, the first of which left the assembly line in August 1943, was based on the Panther ausf D chassis, with modifications that had been incorporated into production up to that time, and fitted with an improved turret. Although much of the new turret was externally similar, a number of important differences were incorporated and these serve as identifying features. The most important and obvious change was the inclusion of a completely re-designed cast cupola for the tank's commander which featured seven periscopes, each protected by an armoured cowling.

In addition, a single periscope for the loader was fitted into the turret roof behind the fume extractor. The interlocking joints of the turret front and side plates were now squared off, whereas those of the Panther ausf D had been dovetailed, and the cast sides behind the

Notes

1. There is little consistency in the names used in official German documents with Panther 1, Panther 2, Panther I and Panther II all being employed at different times.

2. Much of the confusion regarding the names and classifications given to the project is due to the interpretation of captured German documents by Allied intelligence services during the war.

One of the very first Panther ausf D tanks to leave the MAN production lines in early 1943. Points to note are: A. Early pattern Kgs 64/660/150 tracks without ice cleats. B. Initial type drive sprocket. C. First pattern tool rack with Pzkpfw IV towing hook and axe head facing the rear. Very few tanks were fitted with this. D. 16-bolt road wheels. E. Twin Bosch headlights. F. 'Letter box' machine-gun aperture. G. Radio operator's forward-facing periscope, deleted when the Kugelblende entered production. H. Twin gun sight apertures. I. Smoke candle dischargers. J. Early commander's cupola without AA ring fitted from August 1943. K. Turret pistol port. L. Communications hatch. M. Gun cleaning rod tube, here in the open position. N. FuG 5 radio antenna insulator.

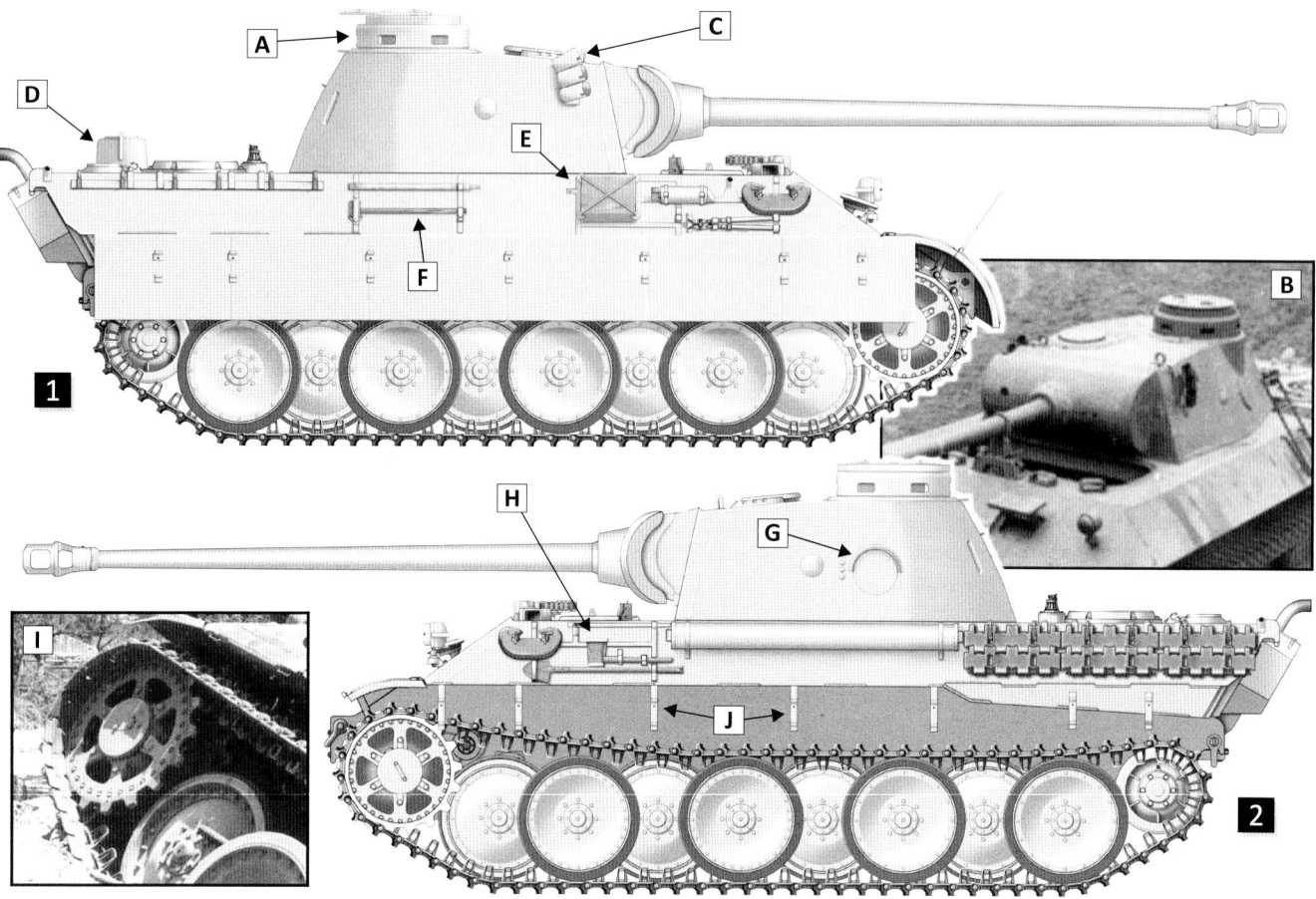

Above: 1. Pzkpfw V Panther ausf D assembled in mid 1943. The most distinctive feature of this model was the simple, cylindrical commander's cupola (A) and the version incorporated into production until August 1943 is shown here. The turret was considerably larger and less angular than that fitted to the Panther-Versuchs V2, the only fully-completed prototype (B), and also lacked the bulge under the cupola. The smoke candle dischargers (C) were discontinued in June and the armoured pot (D) which covered the telescoping air intake tubes was only installed between June and August. A redesigned bracket for the jack block was introduced in May although the cross-strap arrangement shown here (E) continued to be fitted for some time after that. The sledgehammer and track-tensioning tool (F) were added in June 1943. 2. Pzkpfw V Panther ausf D produced after June 1943. The rain channel over the turret communications port (G) was introduced in April 1943 and a number of the 16-bolt road wheels were reinforced with sixteen rivets between June and August. Note that the tank depicted here has a mixture of the 16-bolt and riveted road wheels and this is commonly seen in contemporary photographs. The axe and its bracket (H) were reversed in April 1943. The later-style drive sprocket (I), shown here on both tanks, was certainly being fitted by June 1943 and possibly before that. Compare this with the first production version shown on the previous page. The supports for the hull Schürzen (J) were welded to the underside of the panniers on each side at the assembly plants from April 1943 and units in the field were ordered to add them in the same month.

main gun mantlet were reshaped to accommodate a new type of seal. The hull machine gun was still operated from the rectangular port in the glacis, the so-called 'letter box' opening, which would not be replaced with the Kugelblende mounting until late November or early December 1943. It was at one time thought that this modification was a distinguishing feature of the Panther ausf A, but more than 600 examples of the new tank may have left the factories before its introduction. In fact, this new model was a refinement of the Panther ausf D with the major changes being made to the turret. That this is so is confirmed by the official plan drawings produced by the Heereswaffenamt which clearly state that the new model was made up from a Panther ausf D hull with a Panther ausf A turret.

Production was undertaken by MAN, DB, MNH and also Deutsche Maschinenfabrik Duisburg (DEMAG), which may have assembled as few as fifty tanks. The firm of Henschel und Sohn was contracted to produce the Bergepanther recovery tank. As with the production and assembly of the Panther ausf D tank, the assembly firms were allocated blocks of chassis numbers, or Fahrgestellnummern, and these identified the vehicle throughout its service life. They are noted throughout the text using the abbreviation Fgst Nr.

From January 1943, when the first tank left the assembly line, until May 1945, when the last vehicle was produced, the Panther was subject to a number of modifications, sometimes introduced as economy measures but also as a means of increasing the tank's combat effectiveness and to remedy technical problems that had been identified during trials and in the field. But it should be remembered that new parts were added as they became available and the older versions could be seen for long after the dates given here. The most important changes are listed on the following pages in the month in which they were incorporated and as this section is intended as a spotter's guide, I have omitted many of the internal modifications.

Details of vehicle production and allocation are given on pages 62 and 63.

Another view of the tank shown on page 49. Note the dove-tailed joints of the turret sides and front plate (A) and the aperture for the coaxial machine gun (B). The cross-strap bracket which held the jack block (C) was replaced by a much simplified version in May 1943 but was still fitted for some time after that. Just visible here is the radio operator's forward-facing periscope (D).

January 1943. The first four production model Panther tanks left the assembly lines at MAN, the total output for the month. These vehicles were very similar to the Versuchs-Panther V2, the prototype version, but featured a redesigned turret with a less pronounced hexagonal shape and without the characteristic bulge on the left side under the commander's cupola.

The turret was also fitted with smoke candle dischargers, or Nebelwurfgeräte, and a communications port on the turret left side. Contrary to some accounts the latter were not intended as a shell ejection aperture but rather as a safe means by which the commander could pass messages to any accompanying infantry. Spent shells were disposed of through the turret rear access hatch.

Technical problems were immediately encountered including variations in the turret size and the hull deck which was so uneven that each turret needed to be individually machined and fitted to a particular hull. Furthermore, the turret was unable to traverse without hitting the driver's and loader's hatches when these were in the open position and the gunner could not traverse the turret at all when the tank sat on a slope of greater than 10 degrees. Elevating or depressing the 7.5cm gun caused the mounting bracket to interfere with the T.Z.F.12 gun sight and the recoil guard hit the commander's

seat when the gun was fired. Inadequate ventilation meant that only three rounds could be fired from the 7.5cm gun with the hatches closed.

In the same month, in an effort to increase the tank's armour thickness, experiments with spaced armour plates were conducted but these were eventually abandoned and it was decided that glacis plates made of face-hardened steel be introduced into production by August 1943, presumably with the Panther II model.

February 1943. A base coat of a dark yellow colour, referred to as Dunkelgelb nach Muster, was introduced to replace the dark grey and brown paints then in use.

As the order was dated 18 February, and the total production for that month amounted to just seventeen tanks, only a handful of vehicles could have left the factories in the new colour. Photographs of Panther Fgst Nr.210008, which must have been taken in the second half of February, appear to show a very dark base coat, probably Dunkelgrau RAL 7021 or possibly Rot RAL 8012, a very dark red shade used as a primer. This may suggest, although it is far from conclusive, that it was some time before supplies of Dunkelgelb were available.

Units in the field were issued with supplies of the new shade and also RLM Olivgrün, a Luftwaffe colour, and Rotbraun RAL 8017 with which to camouflage their vehicles. The use of camouflage colours in this period is described in some detail in *TankCraft 30: Tiger I, German Army Heavy Tank, Eastern Front 1942.* In February the Heereswaffenamt directed that, where possible, no modifications should be made to the existing Panther ausf D design as production of the Panther II was expected to begin at some time after May.

March 1943. By the end of the month, over forty-five technical problems requiring change or modification had been identified and the assembly firms were ordered to deliver their completed vehicles to the DEMAG plant at Falkensee where they could be rebuilt.

This order was to come into effect on 3 April 1943 and any tanks assembled before that date were to be used for training. Tanks that had been allocated to operational units were to be retained until new vehicles were available. A total of 121 tanks were modified at the Falkensee plant. The requirement for a face-hardened glacis plate, which was to have entered production in August 1943, was dropped.

April 1943. The holder for the axe mounted on the hull side was reversed. Armoured plates of 5mm thickness, referred to as Schürzen, were mounted on the hull sides to offer greater protection against Russian anti-tank rifles which were capable, at close range, of penetrating the 40mm armour of the lower hull between the wheels and the hull overhang. This simple innovation in fact saved the Panther project at a time when it was suggested that production should be switched to the more heavily armoured Panther II, which was then on the drawing board. In subsequent tests these plates proven to be effective against heavier calibre projectiles although they were never intended to protect the Panther from hollow charge rounds as is often stated. The term Schürzen can be translated as skirts or aprons and they were added to other tanks at about this time including the Pzkpfw IV and Pzkpfw III.

In the same month Dunkelgelb nach Muster, the base camouflage colour, was reclassified as Dunkelgelb RAL 7028 and RLM Olivgrün was replaced by Olivgrün RAL 6003.

............continued on page 55

A Panther ausf D of Panzer-Abteilung 52 captured almost intact after the Kursk battles. Technical details visible here include: A. Tail light and reflector. B. Metal heat shields protecting the rear stowage boxes. Later versions were much simplified. C. Cast armoured exhaust guards. D. The mounting brackets for the 15-ton jack, which has been removed. E. Engine access hatch. F. Cover for starter port. G. Cover for track tensioner, with the right side cover in the open position. H. Armoured cover, sometimes referred to as armoured pot, for submersible gear and snorkel. I. Turret rear access hatch. Another photograph of this tank is reproduced on page 3.

Knocked out during the fighting south of Orel in July 1943, this Panther ausf D of 4.Kompanie, Panzer-Abteilung 51 is fitted with the first pattern drive sprocket, 16-bolt road wheels and commander's cupola without the ring which supported the bracket of the anti-aircraft machine gun. Note the central placement of the handles on the driver's and radio operator's hatches. These were moved to the outside corner, as closed, on later production vehicles and the Panther ausf A. On the turret side, towards the front, is what may be a Panther's head marking which was unusual within this company. Other photographs of this tank show that the company number was not repeated on the turret rear.

A Panther ausf D of 4.Kompanie, Panzer-Abteilung 51 photographed during the early stages of Operation Citadel. Note the large rectangular stowage locker on the hull side behind the jack block. Many, but not all, tanks of Panzer-Regiment von Lauchert were fitted with these boxes and they were almost certainly manufactured at Grafenwöhr before the Panthers left Germany. Note also that the company number has been repeated on the turret rear but apparently without a white outline. This vehicle is also fitted with the first pattern drive sprocket and early 16-bolt road wheels.

This photograph of a Panther ausf D of 7.Kompanie, Panzer-Abteilung 51 provides a clear view of the hull tool rack, driver's and radio operator's periscope armoured covers and smoke candle dischargers. Note the bump stop on the turret front next to the lower edge of the gun mantlet and the method of attaching the Schürzen brackets.

A Panther ausf D of 3.Kompanie, Panzer-Abteilung 51 photographed at some time after August 1943 when the battalion was attached to Panzergrenadier-Division Grossdeutschland. Note the driver's armoured visor in the open position and the twin Bosch headlights. Compare the position of the handles of the radio operator's and driver's hatches with that of Panther 434 shown on the previous page. Another photograph depicting tanks of this company is reproduced on page 6.

............continued from page 52

May 1943. A new bracket for the jack with a single retaining bar was introduced. Heat shields were mounted on the sides of the stowage bins to protect them from the intense heat of the exhaust mufflers. A rain channel was welded over the communications port on the turret left hand side and the escape hatch on the turret rear. The former was later deleted as it was considered to provide an aiming point for enemy anti-tank gunners.

June 1943. Brackets were welded to the hull on the right side to hold a sledgehammer and a track-adjusting tool. In order to provided added structural strength, a rivet was added between each bolt of the 16-bolt road wheels. Despite the modification campaign instituted in late March, many tanks still exhibited serious technical faults and beginning in June a number of Panthers were rebuilt at the Grafenwöhr and Erlangen training facilities. External modifications included a vane sight welded to the turret roof, drain holes cut in the commander's cupola and a rain channel welded over the twin sight apertures on the gun mantlet.

July 1943. The smoke candle dischargers, which had been mounted on the turret sides towards the front, were discontinued from production when it was found that the candles could be ignited by small-arms fire. As an economy measure, a single Bosch headlight was mounted on the left-hand side of the glacis above the fender. Tanks produced up to that time were equipped with two headlights on either side of the glacis. Test conducted using Panther Fgst Nr.212061 showed that the fully submerged vehicle had numerous leaks and this eventually led to the deletion of the submersible equipment.

August 1943. During this month the first three Panther ausf A tanks were completed by MNH at the company's Hanover plant. The communications port on the turret left-hand side was dropped from production. Photographs of Panther Fgst Nr.210137, assembled at MAN in June 1943, show that this modification may have been common for some time. On 24 August the assembly plants were informed that the required fording depth for the Panther would henceforth be reduced from 4 to 1.9 metres. Trials with the available bridging equipment revealed that it could support the Panther's weight and therefore the complicated and expensive submersible arrangement, which included the proposed telescoping air intake pipes which would have allowed the tank to be completely submerged, would no longer be needed.

In addition, the armoured pot covering the submersion gear on the hull rear deck, which had been introduced in June, was dropped from production. Very few tanks were provided with full sets of submersion equipment but those that were seem to have retained it and the armoured cover.

A ring for an anti-aircraft machine gun was added to the commander's cupola and units in the field were also ordered to effect

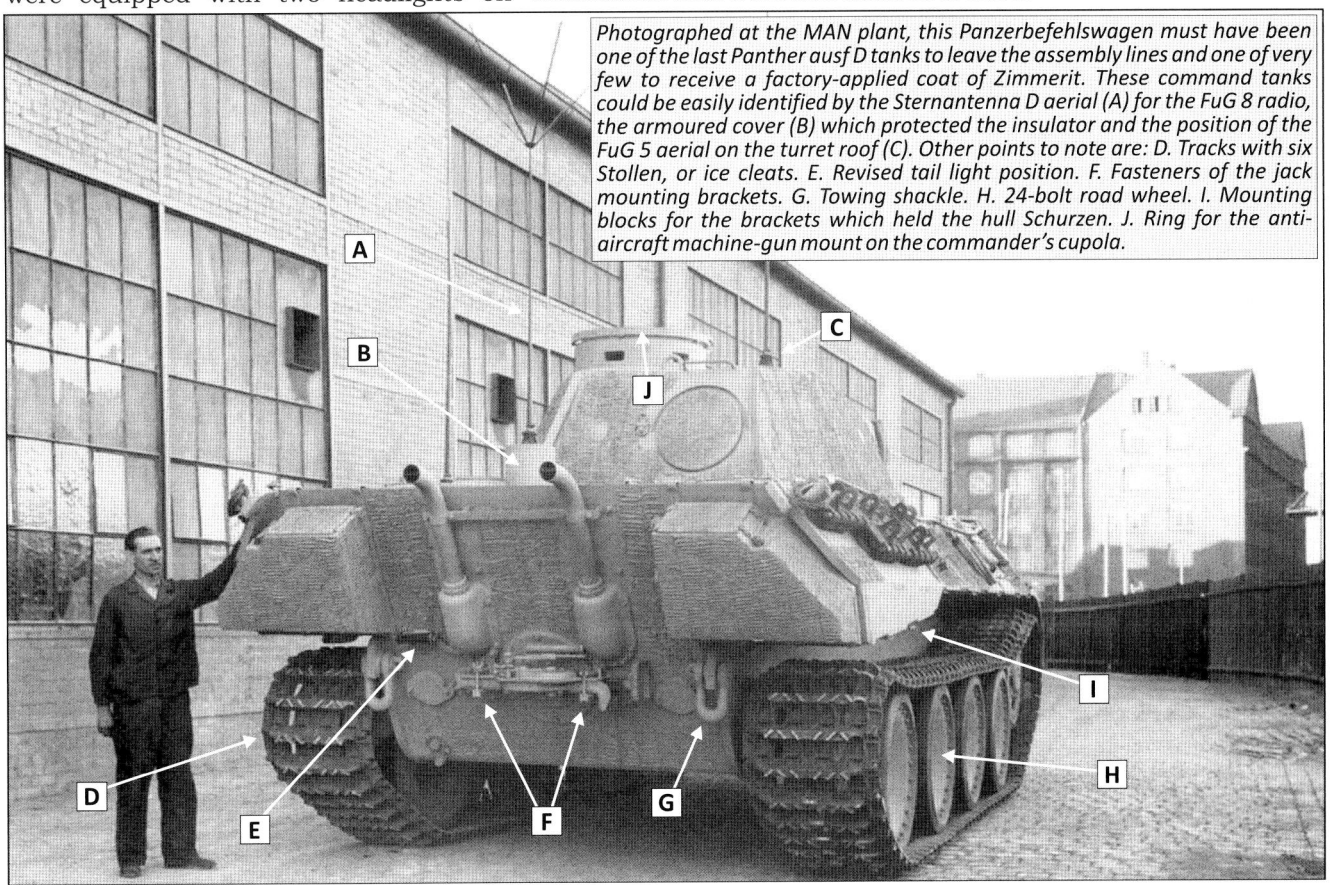

Photographed at the MAN plant, this Panzerbefehlswagen must have been one of the last Panther ausf D tanks to leave the assembly lines and one of very few to receive a factory-applied coat of Zimmerit. These command tanks could be easily identified by the Sternantenna D aerial (A) for the FuG 8 radio, the armoured cover (B) which protected the insulator and the position of the FuG 5 aerial on the turret roof (C). Other points to note are: D. Tracks with six Stollen, or ice cleats. E. Revised tail light position. F. Fasteners of the jack mounting brackets. G. Towing shackle. H. 24-bolt road wheel. I. Mounting blocks for the brackets which held the hull Schurzen. J. Ring for the anti-aircraft machine-gun mount on the commander's cupola.

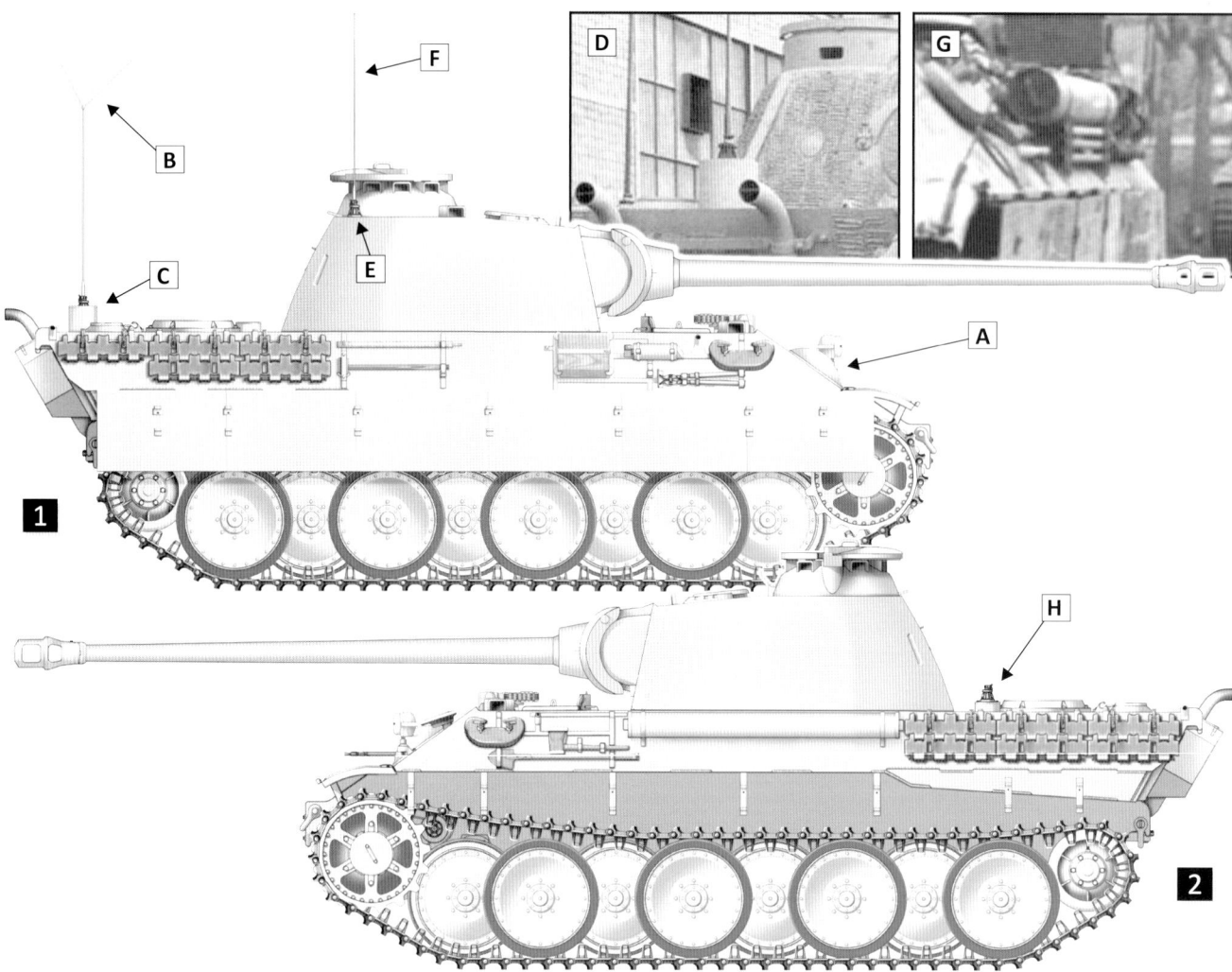

Above: 1. Panzerbefehlswagen (PzBefWg) Panther ausf A. Purpose-built command vehicles were based on all models of the Panther but the vehicle shown here was produced after early November 1943 when the Kugelblende mount (A) was introduced into production. To accommodate the additional radios, and the GG400/12 auxiliary generator which powered them, the ammunition stowage for the main gun was reduced to sixty-four rounds and the coaxial machine gun and its mount were removed. The aperture in the main gun mantlet for the machine gun was filled with a welded plug. In those vehicles based on the Panther ausf A the auxiliary turret traverse mechanism for the loader was deleted but this is of course not visible from the outside. The PzBefWg was fitted with a Funkgerät (FuG) 8 radio which had a range of some 70 kilometres although voice transmissions were usually limited to 25 kilometres. A 1.8-metre Sternantenne D, literally star antenna (B), was mounted on the engine deck and its insulator was protected by an armoured cylinder (C) and this is also shown in our photograph (D). The standard FuG 5 radio was moved to the turret and an insulator (E) and the 2-metre Stabantenne (F) were fixed to the turret roof. This radio provided tank-to-tank communication. On most command vehicles, but not all, three tubes, fixed in a specially-adapted bracket under the cylindrical container for the gun-cleaning rods on the left side of the hull (G), held the Steckmastrohre, or extension masts, which were used to increase the range of the FuG 8 transmitter. It is not uncommon to find standard tanks that were converted to command vehicles by unit workshops and in these the Sternantenna D is often mounted on the hull side. 2. Pzkpfw V Panther ausf A assembled in December when the turret side pistol ports were dropped from production. Note the insulator and antenna for the FuG 5 was fitted in a mount behind the turret (H) on normal production vehicles. Both tanks are fitted with the 24-bolt road wheels introduced from August 1943. Note also the squared-off joints of the turret sides and front plate. All drawings here are shown without Zimmerit for the sake of clarity but most, if not all, Panther ausf A tanks would have received a coating of the anti-magnetic mine paste before leaving the factories.

this change at the same time. New road wheels with twenty-four retaining bolts around the outer edge replaced the earlier 16-bolt wheels and these were supposed to be standard on the Panther ausf A.

Although it was intended that the older wheels would eventually be replaced entirely, the 16-bolt wheels, and those with the reinforcing rivets introduced in the previous June, can still be seen in photographs taken long after this date and many were in fact fitted to the early production Panther ausf A models. The rain channel welded over the sight apertures on the mantlet of the main gun of some of the early Panthers now became a standard fitting.

September 1943. For both models, six chevrons, or Stollen, were cast onto each track link to increase traction in ice and snow. Stocks of the older tracks were still used, however, and it is not uncommon to see both used together. It was ordered that an anti-magnetic mine paste, referred to by its commercial name of Zimmerit, be applied to all vehicles before leaving the assembly plants. The exact date that this order was put into effect is unknown and photographs exist of vehicles completed at the beginning of October that do not have Zimmerit suggesting that some firms at least may have had difficulty obtaining sufficient quantities of the paste. As just thirty-seven tanks were completed in September before production of the

Panther ausf D was halted, it is probable that very few early model tanks would have received factory-applied coatings.

Each of the assembly firms used slightly different methods to apply the coating of Zimmerit paste which resulted in characteristically different textures. There is good evidence that this was done in part to differentiate their product from that of their competitors and this is explained in some detail in *TankCraft 3: Panther Tanks, Germany Army and Waffen-SS, Normandy Campaign 1944* and *TankCraft 32: Panther Medium Tank, IV.SS-Panzerkorps, Eastern Front 1944.*

November 1943. A ball mount for the hull machine gun, the Kugelblende, was incorporated into production. As the new mount contained a sight for the machine gun it was felt that the radio operator's forward-facing periscope was now superfluous and it was no longer fitted. The binocular T.Z.F.12 gun sight was replaced by the monocular T.Z.F.12a version.

Until supplies of single-aperture gun mantlets were available the second, outer sight aperture was sealed with an armoured plug although these vehicles retained the wider rain channel. A number of tanks produced in November and December 1943 were fitted with a towing coupling bolted onto the hull rear plate along the lower edge below the engine access hatch. This was identical to the coupling fitted to the Bergepanther recovery vehicle. As this interfered with ground clearance it was soon dropped from production and although the number of tanks actually fitted with the coupling was small, most Panther ausf A models manufactured up to April 1944 had the necessary brackets and holes, the latter sealed with four bolts.

Units in the field were ordered to apply Zimmerit to those tanks which had not received a coat before leaving the factories.

December 1943. The small pistol ports, referred to as MP Stopfen, on either side of the turret were dropped from production. It was intended that these be replaced by the Nahverteidigungswaffe, or close defence weapon, which was to be mounted in the turret roof, could be traversed through 360 degrees and was capable of firing smoke candles, grenades and flares. A hole was cut in the turret roof, to the right of the cupola, into which the Nahverteidigungswaffe was meant to be fitted but due to difficulties with supply none were available until March 1944 and the turrets of many Panther ausf A models assembled in the interim were instead fitted with a circular plate covering the hole and held in place by four bolts.

Said to depict the crews of II.Abteilung, SS-Panzer-Regiment 5 training in France, this photograph was probably taken in late 1943. If the identification is correct, these tanks may be two of the Panther ausf D vehicles originally allocated to SS-Panzer-Regiment 1 returned as unserviceable, and later shipped to II.Abteilung in November. The tank in the foreground is fitted with the second pattern drive sprocket and a mixture of the 16-bolt and 24-bolt road wheels which would at least date the photograph to some time after August 1943. The right side headlight and its mount appear to have been removed as have parts of the tool rack and the holders for the sledgehammer and track tensioning tool on the hull side. What seems to be a very rough coating of Zimmerit has been applied to parts of the turret and hull. Both tanks are fitted with the early tracks without ice cleats.

From late July 1943 until January 1944, the Panthers of Panzer-Abteilung 51 were controlled by Panzergrenadier-Division Grossdeutschland and were effectively the first battalion of the division's Panzer regiment. The company number, indicating a tank of I.Abteilung headquarters, is visible on the turret side above the stalking panther unit insignia. The latter was not in use during Operation Citadel nor was it employed by the regiment's II.Abteilung as has sometimes been stated. Note the smoke candle dischargers, tool rack, cast mark on the main gun mantlet, Bosch headlight and armoured covers for the radio operator's periscopes. Note also that the bracket holding the wooden jack block appears to be the later version.

This Befehlspanzerwagen Panther ausf D offers a clear view of the antenna extension rack fitted under the gun cleaning rod tube on the hull side. Note how the fender extensions, which were easily lost in service, could be stowed by reversing them and mounting them on the mudguard. This arrangement has often been mistaken for a large fender that was supposedly fitted to early production vehicles.

Although this Befehlspanzerwagen Panther ausf D was photographed in Italy it provides a good view of the rain channel welded above the twin gun sight apertures and the armoured plug fitted to the outside hole. Note that this tank is not fitted with the Sternantenna D and that the hull aerial appears to be in use.

Said to be one of the Panther ausf D tanks of I.Abteilung, SS-Panzer-Regiment 2, this tank has a coat of Zimmerit which was almost certainly applied after the vehicle was shipped from the factory. Note how the pattern on the turret, which is quite neat, differs from that of the hull which could almost be mistaken for mud. Note also that the cupola has also received a coat of the paste and has a field-modified anti-aircraft machine-gun mount.

This Panther ausf A of Panzer-Regiment 2, photographed in late 1943, appears to be a very early production vehicle which is fitted with the binocular gun sight, turret pistol ports, rectangular hull machine-gun aperture, 16-bolt road wheels and has Zimmerit applied to the left front fender only.

From early September 1943 the assembly plants began applying Zimmerit to all tanks before they left the factory. The method of application employed also resulted in a distinct pattern which could, in most cases, identify a particular manufacturer. This is explained in some detail in TankCraft 3: Panther Tanks, German Army and Waffen-SS, Normandy Campaign 1944. The pattern here is indicative of tanks assembled by DEMAG. At least one of the road wheels appears to be the 16-bolt version with additional rivets.

PANTHER PRODUCTION AND ALLOCATION JANUARY-DECEMBER 1943

Month	Type	MAN		Daimler-Benz		Henschel		MNH	
		Qty	Fgst Nr	Qty	Fgst Nr	Qty	Fgst Nr	Qty	Fgst Nr
January 1943	Pzkpfw V ausf D	4	210001-210004	0		0		0	
	Pzkpfw V ausf A								
February 1943	Pzkpfw V ausf D	11	210005-210015	6	211001-211006	0		1	213001
	Pzkpfw V ausf A								
March 1943	Pzkpfw V ausf D	25	210016-210040	14	211007-211020	10	212000-212010	19	213002-213020
	Pzkpfw V ausf A								
April 1943	Pzkpfw V ausf D	0		19	211019-211039	26	212011-212036	39	213021-213059
	Pzkpfw V ausf A								
May 1943	Pzkpfw V ausf D	68	210041-210108	60	211040-211099	25	212037-212061	41	213060-213100
	Pzkpfw V ausf A								
June 1943	Pzkpfw V ausf D	31	210109-210151	40	211100-211139	25	212062-212086	36	213101-213136
	Pzkpfw V ausf A								
July 1943	Pzkpfw V ausf D	58	210152-210209	65	211140-211204	19	212087-212105	48	213137-213184
	Pzkpfw V ausf A								
August 1943	Pzkpfw V ausf D	38	210210-210247	26	211205-211230	15	212106-212120	36	213185-213220
	Pzkpfw V ausf A							3	154801-154803
September 1943	Pzkpfw V ausf D	7	210248-210254	20	211231-211250	10	212121-212130		
	Pzkpfw V ausf A	46	210255-210300	50	151901-151950			45	154804-154848
October 1943	Pzkpfw V ausf D								
	Pzkpfw V ausf A	104	210301-210404	90	151951-152040			50	154849-154898
November 1943	Pzkpfw V ausf D								
	Pzkpfw V ausf A	76	210405-210480	71	152041-152111			75	154899-154973
December 1943	Pzkpfw V ausf D								
	Pzkpfw V ausf A	114	210481-210594	82	152112-152193			60	154974-155033

The Pzkpfw V ausf D and Pzkpfw V ausf A were built by the firms of Maschinenfabrik Augsburg-Nürnberg (MAN), Daimler-Benz (DB), Henschel und Sohn, Maschinenfabrik Niedersachen Hannover (MNH) and Deutsche Maschinenfabrik, almost universally referred to as DEMAG. All tanks were identified by a Fahrgestellenummer (Fgst Nr.), or chassis number, and each company was given a block of these numbers which corresponded to a specific contract. Readers will note that I have not included Fgst Nr. V1 and Fgst Nr. V2, the experimental prototypes or Versuchs-Serie vehicles produced by MAN. Once accepted by the Heereswaffenamt, the army directorate responsible for the research and supply of weapons and ammunition, the tanks were issued to various Heereszeugämtern, or supply offices, which furnished the vehicles with radio equipment, tools and ammunition and also sighted the guns. The Heereszeugämter responsible for the Panther were located at Altengrabow, Grafenwöhr and Sennelager. From there the tanks were allocated to training establishments, test facilities or frontline units as directed by the office of the Inspekteur der Panzertruppen. As can be seen from our chart, the numbers produced only rarely matched the number accepted for a given month. In regard to unit allocations, I have not given definitive figures here for Panzer-Abteilungen 51 and 52 as most of their vehicles were at one time returned to the factories as unsuitable and this is explained further in the unit histories.

PANTHER PRODUCTION AND ALLOCATION JANUARY-DECEMBER 1943

DEMAG (1)		Total	Accepted	Delivered to HZA for issue			Number	Unit
Qty	Fgst Nr	Production	by HWA	Gun tanks	Pz.Bef.Wg	Rebuilds	Allocated	
0		4		4 (2)			3	Heereswaffenamt (3)
		18	18	17 (2)			1	Erprobungsstelle Kummersdorf (4)
		68	59	40 (2)				
		84	78	0				
		194	324	225	10	16	5	Heereswaffenamt (3)
							8	Inspekteur der Panzertruppen
							41	Panzer-Lehrgang Erlangen
							5	Panzertruppen-Schule Wünsdorf
							See text	Panzer-Abteilung 51
							See text	Panzer-Abteilung 52
		132	160	167 (5)	9 (6)	10	8	Panzer-Regiment 39
							40	SS-Panzer-Regiment 1 (7)
							16	SS-Panzer-Regiment 2
		190	202	165	11	4	12	Panzer-Regiment 39
							96(8)	Panzer-Abteilung 51
							31 (9)	SS-Panzer-Regiment 1
		115	120	128	22	3	6	Inspekteur der Panzertruppen
							96	Panzer-Regiment 23
							69	Panzer-Regiment 26
							55	SS-Panzer-Regiment 2
		37	197		3 (10)		17	Inspekteur der Panzertruppen
8	158101-158108	149		152		4	71	Panzer-Regiment 2
							4	Panzer-Regiment 26 (11)
							5	Panzer-Regiment 6
13	158109-158121	257	257	215	19	1	11	Panzer-Regiment 15 (12)
							10	Panzer-Regiment 23
							40	Panzer-Regiment 31
							11	Panzer-Abteilung 51 (13)
							75	SS-Panzer-Regiment 1
							16	Panzer-Regiment 26
10	158122-158131	232	209	212	10		36	Panzer-Regiment 31
							60	Panzer-Abteilung Nord (14)
							96	SS-Panzer-Regiment 1 (15)
							2	SS-Panzer-Regiment 5
							5	SS-Panzer-Regiment 12
							22	Panzer-Regiment 1
11	158132-158142	267	299	291	18		76	Panzer-Regiment 2
							38	Panzer-Regiment 4
							33	Panzer-Regiment 6
							50	Panzer-Regiment 23
							36	Panzer-Regiment 26
							8	Panzer-Regiment 39
							24	SS-Panzer-Regiment 1
							36	SS-Panzer-Regiment 5
							5	SS-Panzer-Regiment 12
							2	Schiess-Schule Putlos
							3	Panzer-Lehrgang Erlangen
							10	Inspekteur der Panzertruppen
							2	Panzer-Reserve OKH

1. The monthly production figures given for DEMAG are estimations based on the numbers of vehicles accepted by the Heereswaffenamt. 2. With the exception of three tanks allocated to Waffen Prüfen 6 (Wa Prüf 6) for testing, all these vehicles were found to be unsuitable. They were returned to the assembly plants, repaired and included in the May 1943 total. 3. Fgst Nr. 210001-210003. These were the Panthers mentioned above as issued to Wa Prüf 6. 4. Fgst Nr. 210004. 5. Fgst Nr. 210125 to 210136 were built by MAN as Bergepanther recovery tanks. 6. Fgst Nr. 210137 was built as a Befehlspanzerwagen but was used as a test vehicle and lacked a number of production features such as pistol ports, tool racks and spare track holders. 7. These tanks had all been returned to the factory by October 1943. 8. These vehicles represented a complete refurbishment. 9. Together with the tanks received in June these vehicles were returned to the factory as unsuitable for front-line use. 10. It is unclear which model was used to build these command vehicles. 11. The August and September numbers for this regiment include two Bergepanther recovery tanks. 12. These tanks were Pzkpfw V ausf D models taken over from Panzer-Abteilung 52. 13. One of these tanks was originally intended for export to Japan. 14. These tanks were all Pzkpfw V ausf D models taken over from SS-Panzer-Regiment 1. 15. These vehicles represented a complete refurbishment.

Dragon Models Ltd
B1-10/F., 603-609 Castle Peak Rd,
Kong Nam Industrial Building,
Tsuen Wan, N. T., Hong Kong
www.dragon-models.com

Tamiya Inc
Shizuoka City, Japan
www.tamiya.com

Trumpeter/Hobby Boss
NanLong Industrial Park, San Xiang,
ZhongShan, Guang Dong, China
www.trumpeter-china.com
www.hobbyboss.com

Academy Plastic Models
521-1, Yonghyeon-dong, Uijeongbu-si,
Gyeonggi-do, Korea
www.academy.co.kr

Hobby Fan/ AFV Club
6F ., No.183, Sec. 1, Datong Rd, Xizhi City,
Taipei County 221, Taiwan
www.hobbyfan.com

Royal Model
Via E. Montale, 19-95030 Pedara, Italy
www.royalmodel.com

Italeri S.p.A.
via Pradazzo 6/b,
40012 Calderara di Reno, Bologna, Italy
www.italeri.com

Takom
www.takom-world.com

Meng-Model
Galaxy Century Bldg., No. 3069 Caitian Rd,
Futian Dist., Shenzhen, Guangdong, China
www.meng-model.com

Amusing Hobby
3-16-19 Ima, Kita-ku, Okayama, Japan
www.amusinghobby.com

Rye Field Models
www.ryefield-model.com
An almost non-existent website. I would
recommend one of the on-line retailers.

Hauler
Jan Sobotka,
Moravská 38, 620 00 Brno,
Czech Republic
www.hauler.cz

Voyager
Room 501, No.411 4th Village,
SPC Jinshan District, Shanghai 200540,
China
www.voyagermodel.com

Griffon Model
Suite 501, Bldg 01, 418 Middle Longpan Rd,
Nanjing, China
www.griffonmodel.com

Aber
ul. Jalowcowa 15, 40-750 Katowice, Poland
www.aber.net.pl

E.T. Model
www.etmodeller.com

Friulmodel
H 8142. Urhida, Nefelejcs u. 2., Hungary
www.friulmodel.hu

Modelkasten
Chiyoda-ku Kanda, Nishiki-Cho 1-7, Tokyo,
Japan
www.modelkasten.com
Very difficult to navigate but worthwhile.

Airfix
www.airfix.com

Theodoros Kalamatas Modelling Worshop
www.facebook.com/Theodoros-Kalamatas-
Modelling-Workshop

Eduard Model Accessories
Mirova 170, 435 21 Obrnice,
Czech Republic
www.eduard.com

Master Club
www.masterclub.ru
It appears that this firm is closely associated
with Armour35, a Russsian mail-order firm.

Model Artisan Mori
Yasutsugu Mori,
Maison Suiryu 302, Kunoshiro-cho 1-10,
Yokkaichi-City, Mie 510-0072, Japan
www.artisanmori.web.fc2.com

Tetra Model Works Co. Ltd.
2F, 18, Dorim-ro 126-gil, Yeongdeungpo-gu,
Seoul, 07299, Korea
www.tetramodel.com

RB Model
Powstancow Wlkp.29B,
64-360 Zbaszyn,
Poland
www.rbmodel.com

M Workshop Singapore
91 Bencoolen St, Sunshine Plaza 01-58,
Singapore
www.themworkshop.com

Zvezda (Zvezda-America)
www.zvezda-usa.com
Note that the Russian catalogue is not the
same as the US version.

ROCHM Model
www.rochmmodel.com
rochmmodel@gmail.com
This company has a huge selection of parts
and accessories for 1/35 scale Panther
models.

In writing this book I referred extensively to Germany's Panther Tank, The Quest for Combat Supremacy *written by the late Thomas L. Jentz with plan drawings by Hilary L. Doyle. Another invaluable resource is Thomas Jentz's* Panzertruppen *books which I would recommend to any reader with an interest in German armour. For the unit histories I relied on a number of sources including* Panzer-Regiment Grossdeutschland *by Hans-Joachim Jung,* Panzer-Regiment 1 *by Wolfgang Schneider and* The Combat History of the 23rd Panzer-Division in World War II *by Dr. Ernst Rebentisch. There are many histories of Operation Citadel available but two I would recommend are* The Battle of Kursk *by David M. Glantz and Jonathan M. House and* The Forgotten Battle of the Kursk Salient *by Valeriy Zamulin. I also relied heavily on the work of Martin Block and the late Ron Klages whose research on vehicle allocations would fill many volumes. I would like to thank the modellers who generously allowed me to publish the images of their work as well as Lisa Hooson and Stephen Chumbley, my editors at Pen & Sword. As always, I am indebted to Karl Berne, Valeri Polokov and J.Howard Parker for their invaluable assistance with the photographs and period insignia.*

Photographed south of Oboyan in July 1943 this Panther ausf D of Panzer-Abteilung 51 is one of the few tanks of 4.Kompanie to carry the snarling panther's head insignia. Although heavily damaged, several early production features are visble including the drive sprocket, 16-bolt road wheels, the mounts for the twin Bosch headlights, smoke candle dischargers, cupola and pistol port.